D0847441

Praise for *Six Sigma for Financial Services*

Every organization must continually strive to address their customers' changing requirements, and learning from the experiences of others can greatly assist us. It's a credit to the authors for bringing so many excellent examples and ideas together in one place. An excellent book for anyone involved in a business process excellence journey!

Paul Baker
Managing Director, Group Operations—Lloyds TSB

Customer service, top-line growth, compliance, and regulatory oversight have all become crucial for financial institutions to thrive in today's competitive environment. Achieving all of them requires aligned organizations and structured processes. The authors masterfully illustrate how Six Sigma and Lean, under a process management umbrella, support these relevant business objectives and how organizations can move along the path of process maturity to internalize these important business tools.

Juan Carlos Paez
Chief Operating Officer—BAC Credomatic Network

Products in financial industries are increasingly homogenous. To differentiate, we need to focus on service excellence grounded on process innovation. Much has been written about Six Sigma in manufacturing industries, but this book provides excellent insights and learning experiences of successful Six Sigma financial organizations. A great reference for those of us who want to "fast-forward" our process innovation initiatives to achieve outstanding results.

Teng Soon Lang
Executive Vice President and Head, Group Quality & Process Innovation—
Overseas Chinese Banking Corporation

The approaches that Hayler and Nichols describe are not just for the Operations function—they apply equally to Marketing and Sales. With its emphasis on stakeholder requirements, strong process governance, and performance measurement, business process excellence is critical for maximizing the return on marketing investments and an organization's value creation.

Arjen Kruger
Former Chief Marketing Officer—MasterCard Europe

SIX SIGMA FOR FINANCIAL SERVICES

How Leading Companies Are Driving Results
Using Lean, Six Sigma, and Process Management

ROWLAND HAYLER
MICHAEL D. NICHOLS

McGraw-Hill

New York   Chicago   San Francisco   Lisbon   London
Madrid   Mexico City   Milan   New Delhi   San Juan
Seoul   Singapore   Sydney   Toronto

The *McGraw·Hill* Companies

Copyright © 2007 by Rowland Hayler and Michael D. Nichols. All rights reserved. Printed in the United States of America. Except as permitted under the United States Copyright Act of 1976, no part of this publication may be reproduced or distributed in any form or by any means, or stored in a data base or retrieval system, without the prior written permission of the publisher.

1 2 3 4 5 6 7 8 9 0   DOC/DOC   0 9 8 7 6

ISBN-13: 978-0-07-147037-7
ISBN-10: 0-07-147037-9

This publication is designed to provide accurate and authoritative information in regard to the subject matter covered. It is sold with the understanding that the publisher is not engaged in rendering legal, accounting, or other professional service. If legal advice or other expert assistance is required, the services of a competent professional person should be sought.
> —*From a declaration of principles jointly adopted by a committee of the American Bar Association and a committee of publishers.*

McGraw-Hill books are available at special quantity discounts to use as premiums and sales promotions, or for use in corporate training programs. For more information, please write to the Director of Special Sales, Professional Publishing, McGraw-Hill, Two Penn Plaza, New York, NY 10121-2298. Or contact your local bookstore.

To my dearest Lizzie, Will, and Em
. . . and to my mother and father
for teaching me there's always
more than one way to do something.

—*RH*

As always, I stand here on the shoulders of those
who come before me,
and honored to have had the chance to help others who follow.

—*MN*

Contents

Foreword

Over the last few years, business leaders across a diverse range of industries and geographies have increasingly recognized and utilized various business process improvement, management, and transformation approaches to achieve better business results. One only has to consider the dramatic increase in the number of books, periodicals, conferences, workshops, and other marketplace offerings on these topics to acknowledge this assertion to be true. So what's driving this increasing level of interest and adoption?

The authors' view—and one that appears to be shared by many business leaders—is that optimally managing business processes in today's global business environment (and that of the future)—characterized by increasingly value-savvy buyers, regulated operating environments, extended supply chains across multiple organizational functions, and third-party partners and suppliers, with many operating across different cultures, time zones, and geographies—has never been more challenging and critical.

The "early adopters" of Six Sigma—giants such as Bank of America, American Express, and Wachovia, to name a few—are realizing millions of dollars of value for their customers and shareholders. These well-documented successes have created a large group of "fast followers"—typically, though not necessarily, smaller banks and financial services institutions such as Countrywide in the United States, Credit Suisse in Europe, ICICI Bank in India, and the Overseas Chinese Banking Corporation in Singapore, which are taking their lead from the early adopters as they look to emulate the big players' use of Six Sigma, Lean, and Business Process Management techniques to achieve significant benefits for their customers and shareholders.

While the increasing interest, popularity, and positive results achieved through the use of these techniques in the financial services industry are clear and well documented, it's also equally clear that the industry has a long way to go to achieve world-class service delivery. Just take a minute to reflect on a service issue (and I use the term *service* loosely!) that you may have recently experienced with your financial services provider. You can probably understand what I am referring to. In fact, the commonly held view among Six Sigma commentators is that the financial services industry is really just at the very beginning of its *required* "world-class" service journey. And yes, it is *required* because in a world where the commoditization of financial services continues apace, service quality is becoming increasingly important as a key differentiator between competing financial services organizations.

It's no surprise therefore, that many observers find this to be a confusing landscape, in the sense that, despite the poor service levels endemic within the financial services industry, many organizations seem to continue to make record year-on-year profits! How can this be, and surely such a situation cannot persist, can it? Additionally, the industry is continuing to see unprecedented levels of consolidation and rationalization with increasing numbers of "local" regional players striving to protect their hard won customer territory, while others are pitching for a stake in the bigger global financial services game. These organizations stand to learn—the hard way—that continuing to operate bad processes—or worse, replicating bad processes on a larger, global scale—will inevitably lead to even greater numbers of dissatisfied customers and value suboptimization for their shareholders.

Clearly the current levels of service quality provided to customers by many financial institutions severely compromise the ability of those institutions to deliver sustainable and meaningful value creation to their shareholders, employees, and business partners, and more broadly, impede the creation of economic prosperity for society at large.

This brings me to the two key objectives of this book. First, it is to fully explore why the world's leading financial services organizations are striving to achieve *sustainable* world-class *business process excellence*. Second and perhaps more importantly, it is to demonstrate how these organizations are now linking the most powerful business process management, improvement, and transformation concepts and methods such as Six Sigma, Lean, and Business Process Management together to improve their results.

In the authors' first book (*"What Is Six Sigma Process Management?"* McGraw-Hill, 2005) they described the "what," "why," and "how" of establishing an end-to-end process perspective and governance approach as the basis for understanding how value is both created, improved, but also lost in organizations. The *process management infrastructure* that they defined in that earlier work now serves as the foundation for a business process excellence approach that enables financial services organizations to identify, prioritize, and eliminate defects and waste through the use of proven business improvement methods.

To achieve the authors' objectives for this book, they share a robust and effective model for defining and achieving business process excellence. They have also included numerous relevant examples, illustrations, and direct practical applications from those organizations that they believe are at the forefront of implementing Six Sigma, Lean, and Business Process Management within the global financial services industry today.

In addition to the many real-life illustrations and stories that the authors have assembled, they also include the results of their research study, conducted at the end of 2005 with senior representatives from 11 financial services organizations, many of whom are leading exponents of Lean, Six Sigma and Business Process Management methods within the industry:

- American Express
- Bank of America
- Credit Suisse
- Dresdner Kleinwort Wasserstein
- First Data Resources
- JPMorgan Chase
- Lloyds TSB
- MBNA Consumer Finance
- Merrill Lynch
- Overseas Chinese Banking Corporation
- UBS

In summary, this book offers readers powerful insights in how to maximize their business transformation and improvement efforts. It provides:

- A thorough understanding of the rationale for business process excellence within the financial services industry today
- A clear and simple structure that enables readers to build their knowledge on how to become a world-class financial services organization
- The opportunity to learn how highly experienced business professionals from a number of leading financial services organizations are applying leading improvement methods
- A highly practical model that can be used to assess and drive your organization's own business process excellence efforts,
- An easy-to-use book for future reference

I highly recommend it as an invaluable guide whether you're just starting, or are looking to expand, your business process excellence efforts. I wish you every success on your continuous journey.

David C. House
Retired Group President
American Express

If you would like to comment on this book or discuss any of the ideas presented, the authors can be contacted at **info@sspm-ideas.com**

Acknowledgments

We would like to take this opportunity to recognize and sincerely thank the following people for their valuable contributions:

Martin Adam, Operational Excellence Process Manager, Credit Suisse; Paul Baker, Group Operations Director, Lloyds TSB; Will Beattie, Business Development Director, IQPC; James Bossert, Senior Program Designer, Quality and Productivity, Six Sigma Deployment, Bank of America; Antony Bream, Vice President, Financial Services, Nimbus Partners; Estelle Clark, Quality Director, UK Financial Ombudsman Service; Richard Collins, Senior Vice President, Business Process Improvement, JPMorgan Chase Home Finance; Laura Currier, Senior Vice President, Fidelity Employer Services Company, Fidelity Investments; Robin Davies, Managing Director, Venturehaus; Alexis Goncalves, Global Director, Global Quality Intelligence, Citigroup (Consumer Bank); John Gilbert, Global Head of Process Excellence, Operations, UBS; Dominic Hirsch, Managing Director, Retail Banking Research; David C. House, Retired Group President, American Express; Steve Kirby, Director, Merrill Lynch Investment Managers; Nayan Kisnadwala, Chief Financial Officer, MBNA Consumer Finance; Arjen Kruger, former Chief Marketing Officer, MasterCard Europe; Jim Li, former Executive Vice President of Global Six Sigma, American Express; Carlos Lozano, Business Improvement Director, EMEA, First Data Resources (Europe); Reg May, Independent Management Consultant and former Deputy Chief Executive, Access Credit Card Company; Guy Noble, Head of Group Service and

Sigma Improvement, Lloyds TSB; **Juan Carlos Paez**, Chief Operating Officer, BAC Credomatic Network; **Pete Pande**, President, Pivotal Resources; **William E. Rinehart**, Vice President and Chief Risk Officer, Ocwen Financial; **Roberto M. Saco**, Vice President, Strategic Planning, American Express; **Helen Smith**, Head of Process Improvement, Marks & Spencer Money; **Teng Soon Lang**, Executive Vice President, Quality and Process Innovation, Overseas Chinese Banking Corporation; **Ernst Verbeek**, Regional Vice President, First Data International (western Europe); **Greg Watson**, Managing Partner, Business Systems Solutions Inc.; **Jack West**, Ph.D., Past President of the American Society for Quality; **Adam Wheelwright**, Global Head of Securities Process Delivery, Dresdner Kleinwort Wasserstein; **Andy Wright**, Vice President, Global Network Services Business Solutions, EMEA, American Express; **Janet Young,** Managing Partner, Change Edge Consulting, LLC.

We would also like to thank the following people for their generous assistance:

Teri Charest, US Bancorp; **Paige Chesser**, Bank of America; **Mary Eshet**, Wachovia; **Michael F Fusco**, JPMorgan Chase; **Cyndi Koh**, Development Bank Singapore; **Tim Lubinsky**, Bank of America; **Linda Ludwig**, Ocwen Financial; **Michael Maze**, Graphics Designer; **Sierk Nawijn**, ABN Amro; **John Oliver**, GE; **Emma Rees,** Barclays; **Tony Ridley**, HSBC; **Tara Rio**, Countrywide; **Fay Spano**, American Society for Quality; **Judy G. Tinzer,** American Express; **Jonathan Woodyer**, Citigroup.

Without the contribution and assistance of the people acknowledged here, this book would not have been possible.

1

Today's Financial
Services Landscape

Introduction

The current global financial services industry is characterized by significant change and complexity, perhaps more so than at any other time in its relatively short history. Many factors are driving these changes and shaping the operating landscape of today and subsequently tomorrow. Unquestionably, those organizations that will prosper and ultimately "win" in such complex and challenging environments are those that can offer "buyers" something radically different. Some commentators believe that a new "killer" product or service offering may become the unique differentiator; others believe it's the "customer experience" that ultimately shapes buyers' habits and their loyalty to a company's brand and its resultant success. The truth is that buyers, whether consumers, small- to medium-size enterprises, or global corporations, value both; and the delivery of both requires seamless execution in increasingly challenging operating environments, each and every day.

In Part 1 of our book, we will:

- Introduce the *key terms and operational definitions* that will be used throughout, to ensure a common understanding
- Describe the *emerging trends and driving forces of change* within the industry that now require financial services organizations to radically rethink their approaches to service quality
- Share *real-life success stories from some of the leading financial services organizations* that use Six Sigma, Lean, and Business Process Management methods today

- Introduce *world-class business process excellence* and question its meaning within the context of today's financial services landscape

In addressing these topics, we hope to provide a comprehensive picture of the challenges and opportunities that exist within the financial services industry today. This will serve as the context for the subsequent parts of our book in which we will explore how Six Sigma, Lean, Process Management, and other business process improvement methods can be successfully assembled and used to drive results.

CHAPTER

Key
Definitions

L ET'S START with some key terms and operational definitions
that we'll use throughout this book.

Six Sigma, Lean, and Business Process Management

What do we mean by the terms *Six Sigma, Lean, and Business Process Management?*

Six Sigma concepts originated at the Motorola Corporation in the
United States in the mid-to-late 1980s and were subsequently
expanded at GE and other leading firms during the 1990s. Over the last
15 years or so, Six Sigma has been increasingly recognized as a powerful approach to achieve business process improvements in both manufacturing and, more recently, service and transactional industries.

Six Sigma was initially founded on principles of fact-based decision
making and the application of scientific management methods, but it
actually integrates many different creative, technical, and change management methods, tools, and techniques to improve business processes.
The focus of Six Sigma is a detailed understanding of customer
requirements, coupled with the use of facts and data to reduce process
variation, thereby enabling organizations to deliver consistent, high-
quality services to customers. While many people initially think that

Six Sigma is all about statistics, the organizations that are most successful with their Six Sigma efforts recognize that it's a lot more than that, although the use of advanced statistical tools *can* have a key role to play.

Today there are many different definitions of Six Sigma. The definition we like best[1] and will use throughout this book characterizes Six Sigma as:

- A *measure* to define the capability of a process—the sigma symbol (σ) is a letter from the Greek alphabet used to signify standard deviation.[2]
- A *goal* for improvement that reaches near perfection—3.4 defects per million opportunities (DPMO). A *defect* is defined as an output that fails to meet a customer requirement.
- A *system of management* to achieve lasting business leadership and top performance—utilizing improve, design-redesign, and process management methodologies.

Lean concepts originated in Japan in the 1950s–1980s and are embodied in the Toyota Production System, a widely recognized and respected approach to manufacturing production. Lean was adopted by many organizations globally in the 1990s, mostly in manufacturing, where it was used as a rapid problem-solving approach. Increasingly it's being successfully used in service and transactional environments—including financial services.

Lean was founded on the principles of *optimal process design* and *pull-based processing*. Its primary initial emphasis is on the reduction of waste and cycle time. In fact, the basic idea of Lean is that anything that doesn't add value for the customer is waste. Seven types of waste have been identified:

1. Excess motion (ergonomic or physical)
2. Excess transportation (logistics, shipping)
3. Waiting time
4. Defects and rework (correction of errors)
5. Overproduction and obsolescence
6. Excess processing or work (or inspection)
7. Excess inventory

Today the most widely used Lean core concepts are those of:

Value. Identifying the value of each activity, eliminating non-value-adding activities, and optimizing value-adding work

Flow. Aligning capacity with demand so that the product or service flows at the right speed

Pull. Designing information and ordering processes so that actual customer orders trigger production as opposed to forecasts

Perfection. Systematizing the management of processes to deliver optimum customer value

Business Process Management (BPM) emerged as a business phenomenon in the late 1990s and appears to have its origins in the domain of software application integration. Although the term continues to be used by a number of technology vendors to describe their products, the term is now becoming more broadly defined as the thought processes around the concept of BPM mature. In essence, its definition is moving away from a description of technical tools and functionality and toward a holistic view of BPM as a business practice and management discipline.

The simplest definition of BPM we've found, and that we intend to use throughout our book, is from a Gartner Research Note:

> *BPM is a management practice that provides for governance of a business's process environment toward the goal of improving agility and operational performance. BPM is a structured approach employing methods, policies, metrics, management practices and software tools to manage and continuously optimize an organization's activities and processes.[3]*

In summary, our view is that all the above methods are complementary. They can and should coexist with one another. Together they offer the most powerful mix of approaches to address the kinds of issues and opportunities that financial services organizations face today. The bottom line is that organizations need to use a combination of methods and tools to optimize their performance and create value.

How are we defining *financial services*?

In the simplest sense, we can think of today's financial services industry as an overarching industry with three major sectors, each focusing on the development and delivery of specific products and services. The sectors (used to create listings such as the Fortune 500[4]) are based on categories established by the U.S. Office of Management and Budget.

Organizations often offer products that cut across different sectors, and so they are listed in the sector from which they derive their greatest volume of revenues. The three sectors are:

- *Commercial and savings banks.* This sector includes such organizations as Citigroup, HSBC, Bank of America, Credit Suisse, and JPMorgan Chase. Organizations in this sector offer a very wide range of products and services, from consumer checking and current accounts, mortgage and loan products, unsecured lending, and credit cards to commercial lines of credit, funding for mergers and acquisitions, and brokerage services.
- *Diversified financials.* This sector is much smaller in comparison with the above sector and includes organizations such as GE, American Express, and Countrywide Financial Corporation. As the name suggests, organizations in this sector offer a diverse range of products and services such as credit cards, travel services, and leasing finance. Typically these organizations tend to operate under more limited banking licenses.
- *Securities.* This sector is the smallest sector and includes only a few organizations, such as Morgan Stanley, Merrill Lynch, and Goldman Sachs. These organizations provide offerings for private, institutional, and government clients, including mutual fund, insurance, annuity, trust, and clearing services, in addition to the more traditional investment banking and brokerage services.

There are also four insurance sectors (covering mutual and stock), including such leading companies as AXA, ING, Prudential, Met Life, Allianz, AIG, and Zurich Financial Services. In addition, organizations that provide specialized products and services, primarily to enable the financial services industry, appear in a number of other industry categories. For example, First Data[5] is listed within the computer and data services sector.

Although we will include occasional references to organizations from the insurance sector and enabling organizations such as First Data, the focus of our book will be on the core financial services sectors—commercial and savings banks, diversified financials, and securities.

How do we define a *business process*?

There are many different ways in which we can define a business process. Perhaps a good place to start is with a definition by Michael Hammer, taken from a white paper he wrote for the Microsoft Corporation. Here's what he had to say:

> *The term "business process" is both overused and misunderstood. On the one hand, it is often employed in a loose fashion, simply to refer to any work activity. On the other, it is sometimes confused with the unrelated notion of procedure.*
>
> *In fact, the process concept has a precise and simple definition: **a process is end-to-end work**, in contrast to piecemeal work.... Formally, a process is an organized group of related activities that work together to create customer value.*[6]

We particularly like that definition because of its emphasis on *customer value* creation, a concept often overlooked by many financial services companies. You might share our view that as customers, we sometimes feel the organizations' operations are designed to maximize their value creation at the expense of delivering value to us, their customers.

In our first book,[7] we described the importance of *end-to-end core processes*—the high-level processes that are the primary drivers of value, customer satisfaction, and profit for any organization. Understanding end-to-end core processes in any organization is a starting point for developing a process model that enables organizations to identify important internal and external functional connections and interfaces. We'll explore this further in Chapter 9. So to recap—for now we can define a business process as *end-to-end work that creates customer value*.[8]

Finally, what do we mean by the term *business process excellence*?

We shall use this relatively new term extensively throughout our book, and thus it warrants definition here. In fact, the concept we're about to define has tended to have been overcomplicated by others in the past, so we'll do our best to keep our definition simple.

If we take our definition of a business process—*end-to-end work that creates customer value*[9]—and consider for a moment what organizations actually need in order to continually "create customer value" from their "end-to-end work," we might identify two distinct but interrelated components.

First, organizations need to continually understand what their customers truly value and, based on that knowledge, set appropriate performance goals and evaluate how their end-to-end processes are doing in delivering that value (i.e., meeting or, where appropriate, exceeding their customers' changing requirements). So in this regard, we can think of *business process excellence* as a means by which organizations can understand their customers' requirements and, based on that information, set appropriate goals and track performance. For example, this may require the organizations' processes to achieve Six Sigma (6σ) levels of performance by eliminating defects (see Figure 1.1). Or it may require them to achieve world-class levels of *process cycle efficiency*—the percentage of total cycle time spent on value-added activities—generally accepted to be about 50 percent in a service and transactional environment.

Second, where organizations find that their process performance is not currently delivering value to their customers, or will be unable to in the future (in Six Sigma, this is known as *process entitlement*), they need to apply the appropriate methods, tools, and techniques to improve those processes.

σ	DPMO	Yield
6	3.4	99.9997%
5	233	99.977%
4	62,210	99.379%
3	66,807	93.32%
2	308,537	69.2%
1	690,000	31%

Figure 1.1   What is Six Sigma performance?

The methods, tools, and techniques that organizations use could be Six Sigma, Lean, Business Process Management, Kaizen,[10] Workout,[11] or any other, depending on the situation. The important point is that organizations apply the correct approaches, at the correct time, in the correct way to ensure that their business processes meet their customers' requirements and provide continuing value. So in this regard, we can think of *business process excellence* as a means by which organizations can utilize the most appropriate methods, tools, and techniques to meet—*and* where value creating for both customers *and* shareholders, exceed—customers' requirements.

In our experience many organizations, and financial services organizations in particular, have a tendency to focus on the methodology—"Let's launch Six Sigma!"—without really understanding, as well as they should, what their customers truly value. In these circumstances, organizations often wonder why they continue to lose revenue-generating customers to the competition or why they fail to see improvements in their customer satisfaction scores. It's often because they're not working on the things that matter most to their customers—the things that *customers truly value*.

These ideas might sound a little bit familiar. We really wish we could tell you they're new, but they're not. In fact, our definition of *business process excellence* has its origins firmly rooted in many business improvement approaches that numerous organizations have used and continue to use today: a lineage that includes Total Quality Management, Operational Excellence, Business Process Management, ISO9000, Six Sigma, Lean, Kaizen, and Workout, to name those that you might be more familiar with. Incidentally, *business process excellence* is *not* a term for a software solution. We mention this because if you were to run a Google search on the term, you'd end up with over 100,000 hits, many of which relate to software and technology vendors—it seems they really like the term!

To summarize, business process excellence is both a goal and an overarching framework that enables financial services organizations to apply whatever methods, tools, and techniques they consider most appropriate (regardless of name, origin, or lineage) to transform and continually improve their business. We firmly believe that in order to significantly improve business performance on a sustainable basis, financial services organizations will need to be continually mindful of both the *what* and the *how* of *business process excellence*.

Notes

1. P. Pande, R. Neuman, and R. Cavanagh, *The Six Sigma Way* (McGraw-Hill, New York, 2000).
2. A measure of the average distance that values deviate from the mean, or the arithmetic average.
3. M. Melenovsky, J. Sinur, J. Hill, and D. McCoy, "Business Process Management: Preparing for the Process-Managed Organization," Gartner RAS Core Research Note G00129461.
4. www.CNNMoney.com.
5. First Data is one of the top processors of bank card transactions in the United States. It provides its processing and portfolio management products and services to more than 1,400 financial institutions and other issuers of credit, debit, private label, oil, and other cards, including stored-value and smart cards. *Source:* www.hoovers.com.
6. M. Hammer, "Business Processes in Financial Services," Microsoft white paper (September 2003). Hammer is also the coauthor of *Reengineering the Corporation: A Manifesto for Business Revolution* (HarperCollins, New York, 1993).
7. R. Hayler and M. Nichols, *What Is Six Sigma Process Management?* (McGraw-Hill, New York, 2005).
8. For a fuller definition and characterization of a business process, we recommend *Business Process Management: The Third Wave* by Howard Smith and Peter Fingar (Meghan-Kiffer Press, Tampa, FL, 2002). This builds upon the excellent work of Tom Davenport in his landmark book entitled *Process Innovation.*
9. Our working definition of *value* is that it's a combined function of both *quality* and *price as perceived by the buyer.*
10. *Kaizen* is a Japanese term meaning "gradual unending improvement by doing little things better and setting and achieving increasingly higher standards."
11. Workout is a powerful decision-making approach for getting frontline employees who face operational and tactical challenges in the business to enthusiastically and energetically engage in addressing them. It uses a three-phase process that consists of scoping sessions, intense highly facilitated action planning sessions, and implementation.

The Driving Forces of Change

NOW THAT WE'VE INTRODUCED some basic definitions, we would like to turn our attention to the *key driving forces of change* that we believe exist within the financial services industry today—and that require organizations to achieve business process excellence in order to successfully compete.

Before launching into increasing levels of detail, let's just take a few minutes to consider the big picture. What is it that organizations (regardless of their industry) should continually be striving to achieve? We believe that, at its simplest, it is to:

- Create compelling new product and service offerings
- Provide service quality and value as defined by customers
- Generate attractive returns for shareholders
- Be the best place to work for employees
- Operate mutually value-creating partnerships with third-party suppliers
- Act with ethical, social, and environmental responsibility

As we consider the trends that impact upon the ability of financial services organizations to address the above, we thought it simplest to organize our thinking around two broad categories. In the first category, we will explore the requirements of a financial services organization's key stakeholders—customers, shareholders, and regulators.[1] In the second category, we will explore emerging trends in relation to operational execution—specifically, scale and complexity, extended enterprise, and technology enablement and acceleration—and the implication of each of these on meeting the requirements of key stakeholders.

Let's start with customer satisfaction—a key stakeholder requirement.

Key Driver #1: The Need to Continually Satisfy Customers

Why is the need to continually satisfy customers driving the business process excellence agenda in many organizations today? After all, isn't ensuring customer satisfaction something that organizations have been doing for decades?

Well, perhaps, but just take a few minutes to consider this verbatim transcription[2] of a phone conversation between a customer and a telephone call center (TCC) representative at a leading financial services company.

TCC representative:	Hello, this is XYZ Bank. How can I help you?
Customer:	Hello, this is Mr. Smith. My account number is 12345678.
TCC representative:	Hello, Mr. Smith. Before we can proceed, I'll need to ask you a few security questions. Can you please tell me your date of birth and mother's maiden name?
Mr. Smith:	Yes, it's 11/08/87, and my mother's maiden name is Brown.
TCC representative:	Thank you, Mr. Smith. That's fine. How can I help you today?
Mr. Smith:	I'd like to give you some money by debit card, please.
TCC representative:	I see. Well I'm afraid you can only pay that way if you're in arrears, and I can see that your account is up to date.

Mr. Smith:	OK, can I pay by credit card?
TCC representative:	I'm sorry. We don't accept credit card payments to that type of account.
Mr. Smith:	OK. Can I go to a bank and pay three months in advance, because I'm going on a long vacation.
TCC representative:	I'm sorry. We don't have a facility to do that.
Mr. Smith:	Oh!
TCC representative:	Is there anything else that I can help you with today?
Mr. Smith:	Er, no.
TCC representative:	OK. Well, thank you for calling XYZ Bank, and have a nice day!

Unfortunately, these kinds of customer experiences are not unique. In fact, you may well have experienced something similar (or worse!) yourself. If we were to dissect this call, we could ask many questions about this interaction, or "moment of truth," as such experiences are often described. It seems to us that the most basic questions are these:

1. Did the interaction create value for Mr. Smith, the customer? *No.*
2. Did it create value for XYZ Bank? *No. In fact it cost the bank money to handle the call, although the TCC manager might be pleased that the call only took 60 seconds versus a target time of 180 seconds per call.*
3. Did it create value for the TCC representative? *Unlikely. It's not the kind of call that motivates employees.*
4. Did it create value for anyone? *No, although possibly—just possibly—it might have made a regulator happy.*
5. Is Mr. Smith likely to be more loyal to XYZ Bank as a result of this interaction? *Extremely unlikely—well, if you were Mr Smith, would you now be more loyal?*

If we were to look more closely at the interaction, we might conclude that Mr. Smith was actually being very reasonable and was simply attempting to conduct his financial affairs in a responsible way. Yet however reasonable this request may appear, on this occasion it was beyond the ability of XYZ Bank to meet Mr. Smith's requirements.

So how, in such a saturated financial services market (incidentally the above example is based on a conversation that took place with a U.K. financial services organization) can this be possible? It seems the key problem here is that XYZ Bank has failed to look at this particular transaction process from a customer's point of view, and in the absence of this perspective, the bank is failing to understand what creates value for Mr. Smith—and, indeed, for XYZ Bank. It may seem obvious to state that understanding the customer experience is a key factor in achieving business process excellence, but it's often the case that financial services organizations don't fully understand their customers' service experiences to the extent that they should.

In fact, analyzing and synthesizing such continually changing experiences as a foundation from which segmented customer requirements can be fully understood and "hardwired" into the ways in which processes are executed are often extremely difficult. Six Sigma methods and tools, such as Kano Analysis, Quality Function Deployment (don't be put off by the quality-nerd name—it's a great tool!), and Conjoint Analysis offer proven approaches for doing just this. We'll describe these more in Chapter 12. Of course, if achieving business process excellence were easy, financial services organizations would probably be doing it already.

A highly successful approach to improving levels of customer satisfaction has been taken by Wachovia Corporation, a large financial services company that provides a broad range of banking, asset management, wealth management, and corporate and investment banking products and services. It is one of the largest providers of financial services in the United States, operating as Wachovia Bank in 16 states from Connecticut to Florida and west to Texas, and operates as Western Financial through 19 branches in southern California.

WACHOVIA

Wachovia[3] recognized the need to better understand what customers were experiencing, and with this in mind, it established a customer experience program. The objectives of the program were to (1) provide unmatched service and advice, (2) satisfy its customers' needs, and (3) support its customers' ongoing success. Wachovia started by defining *customer loyalty* in terms that could be understood and, very importantly, measured, as a means to engage employees at all levels of the organization:

- **Increased loyalty yields**

  - More business
  - Relationship longevity
  - "Benefit of doubt" on service breaks

- **What does this mean for you?**

  - Increase in sales ... revenue ... profit ... value to the stockholders

- **How do you measure loyalty?**

  - Overall satisfaction
  - Likelihood to continue doing business
  - Likelihood to recommend

The efforts were, and continue to be, focused on translating the *voice of the customer* (known in Six Sigma as *VOC*) into critical-to-quality features (known in Six Sigma as *CTQs*) that the bank can execute against. This involved capturing the voice of the customer, analyzing and assessing that information to truly understand customers' critical-to-quality requirements, and then using that information to make improvements to the bank's processes.

Written in this way, Wachovia's journey sounds very straightforward. In truth it rarely is, but Wachovia has remained focused on its program objectives, and it's really paid off. The bank has benefited from some highly impressive improvements in its customer satisfaction scores[4] (up from 5.59 to 6.63) and associated levels of customer attrition (down from 20 to 12 percent—see Figure 2.1). Improving customer satisfaction increases customer loyalty, and so it's no surprise that the customer loyalty results[5] are equally impressive.

In our view, it's unlikely to be a coincidence that Ken Thompson, chairman and CEO of Wachovia, recently reported that 2005 was "a year of strong performance,"[6] with the corporation's key achievements including:

- Increased earnings of 16 percent from "combined" 2004:

  - Operating EPS up 9 percent from 2004
  - Fourth consecutive year of double-digit earnings growth

- Led customer service among major bank peers—record customer service and customer loyalty scores

- Superior shareholder returns:
  - Four-year total return of 92 percent
    - Number 1 of the top 20 banks
    - Fifth straight year of returns outperforming median of top 20 banks
  - Increased dividend of 17 percent from 2004, reflecting strong earnings growth; payout ratio remains in the 40–50 percent range

Of course, when financial services organizations fail to meet their customers' requirements, their shareholders are unlikely to receive the kinds of returns that Wachovia's shareholders enjoy—certainly not on such a sustained basis. When customers' requirements are not met, customers respond in different ways. Some might stop using the product altogether, some might significantly curtail their usage, some might choose to complain, while others may simply become increasingly indifferent. In any event, it's extremely rare that a failure to meet customers' requirements results in greater customer loyalty!

Let's consider this observation on the subject of customer loyalty made by IBM Consulting Services in 2002:

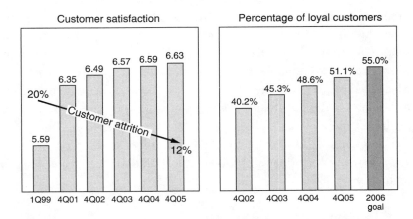

Figure 2.1 Improving customer satisfaction increases loyalty.
Source: Wachovia

As customers have become more aware of their financial services needs, they have also become more willing to shop around for the best deals. This is leading to a marked decline in customer loyalty. While customers seldom desert their traditional suppliers totally, they increasingly look elsewhere for their new banking, insurance and investment needs. This shift toward multiple providers is costing FI's [Financial Institutions] valuable incremental business and threatening their share of wallet.[7]

Since that time, new entrants continue to sharpen customer expectations as the entrants compete aggressively on price (e.g., consider the significant share shift occurring on consumer credit card receivables in many markets around the world). In the United States, Web sites such as Quicken.com have made it easier for consumers to shop around; for example, consumers can search for credit cards using criteria such as introductory offers, APR, rewards, and annual fees. This sharpening of customer expectations has significant implications both for customer retention and for the image of financial services organizations when those expectations are not met.

In a number of markets, the customers of financial services organizations now have recourse to an ombudsman service if they believe their service grievances are inappropriately addressed by their financial services organization. For example, in the United Kingdom, the Financial Ombudsman Service was set up by law as an independent public body. Its job is to resolve individual disputes between consumers and financial services firms—fairly, reasonably, quickly, and informally. It appears that its staff members have been rather busy lately. Consider this extract from the Chief Ombudsman's report covering the period April 2003 to March 2004:

By any measure, this year has been one of exceptional activity for the Financial Ombudsman Service. During the year we received—and resolved—more complaints than ever before. In the four years since we brought our predecessor dispute-resolution schemes together under one roof, we have seen our workload almost quadruple. This year alone, the number of new complaints reaching the ombudsman service increased by 57% on the previous year (which itself saw a 44% annual increase).

> *This significant rise has been driven by the flood of endowment com-*
> *plaints—from under 15,000 last year to over 50,000 this year. Neither*
> *we nor the financial services industry—which we consult on our work-*
> *load estimates—had forecast a surge on such a major scale.*[8]

In response to this surge in complaint volume, the service introduced a range of initiatives, including:

- Adopting new case-handling procedures
- Taking a more flexible approach to managing caseloads
- Finding new ways of moving and reallocating resources
- Recruiting almost a hundred more new staff

In fact, one of the more recent staff to be recruited is Estelle Clark,
a highly experienced Six Sigma practitioner who, in the role of quality
director, is leading the implementation of Lean Six Sigma techniques
at the Financial Ombudsman Service. This is a key appointment, not
only for the Financial Ombudsman Service, but also for the broader
U.K. financial services industry. It sends a clear message that Lean Six
Sigma techniques are increasingly valued in the industry. We believe it
would be a very good move for other such bodies within the industry,
including those responsible for regulatory compliance, to make similar
such appointments.

Not all complaints end up as a case at a Financial Ombudsman's Service—the majority don't; as consumers we typically just tolerate bad
service because there's often no alternative. In fact, the general level of
inertia and apathy toward changing financial services providers—especially for mortgages and home loans, less so with credit cards—is costing consumers, collectively, millions upon millions of dollars each year,
and financial services organizations are literally "laughing all the way to
the bank!"

So what's the big deal about complaints? We complain about things
all the time—some more than most. We complain because our requirements are not met (as previously described, failure to meet a customer
requirement is referred to as a *defect* in Six Sigma). The big deal is that
failing to meet customers' requirements increasingly carries consequences for financial services organizations. It can be very costly, not
just in terms of lost customers (both existing and prospective), but also

increasingly in terms of fines and associated bad press coverage in the marketplace. This is especially so where the complaints are about compliance-related failures.

Consider this recent report in a leading U.K. newspaper:

Abbey Fined £800,000 for Mishandling Mortgage Complaints
By James Moore, Financial Correspondent
(*SUNDAY TELEGRAPH*—LONDON—MAY 29, 2005)

Abbey National was yesterday fined £800,000 by the City watchdog for mishandling complaints about endowment mortgages.

The Financial Services Authority said that between October 2001 and September 2003 the banking group failed to properly deal with 5,000 complaints about endowments, including 3,500 that were rejected when they should have been upheld.

The regulator said that based on industry averages, the 3,500 could have lost up to £19m in compensation. During the period under investigation, Abbey rejected 93 [percent] of the 20,444 cases it had made decisions on.

Abbey said it would revisit 50,000 endowment complaints it had rejected, as a result of the watchdog's investigation. It said it was too early to say how much this would cost, but admitted that it might have to increase the £204m [million] of provisions it has made to cover various liabilities, including mis-selling claims.

The bank was bought for £9.6 billion last November by Spain's Banco Santander, but the company said the problems dated from before that. Abbey owns life insurers Scottish Mutual, Scottish Provident and Abbey National Life which all issued endowments.

Abbey said it fully accepted its complaints handling was inadequate during the period highlighted by the FSA and took the ruling "extremely seriously." The regulator said it had given Banco Santander credit for co-operating with its inquiries and quickly agreeing the facts of the case to enable an early settlement.

The FSA said the penalty—the highest imposed for mishandling endowment complaints—would have been higher had the bank not co-operated.

FSA director of retail markets Clive Briault said: "By putting its own interests ahead of those of its customers with a mortgage endowment complaint, Abbey has singularly failed to treat its customers fairly. Its failings were made more serious as they occurred at a time when there was a high level of awareness within the industry about mortgage endowments and concerns regarding the fair handling of complaints."

Abbey was also criticized for supplying misleading information to the regulator in response to one of its "dear chief executive" letters about endowment complaints from the FSA chief executive John Tiner.

The watchdog's ruling relates only to complaints about policies sold by Abbey's own advisers. People with policies from Scottish Mutual or Scottish Provident that were sold to them by independent financial advisers should raise complaints with their advisers rather than Abbey.

Harsh words indeed and hardly a glowing endorsement of this financial services organization's commitment to its customers. Interestingly, Abbey has only just started to introduce Six Sigma—and as far as we're aware, it had not introduced it at the time this case occurred. We wonder if such a situation would have arisen had the bank been utilizing the voice-of–the-customer methods, tools, and techniques that are integral to a Six Sigma approach. Not only does the above case highlight the need for a much stronger customer focus, but it also highlights the impact—such that it can be directly measured—on shareholder value creation.

As Christian Poirier, senior executive vice president of the Strategy and Marketing Division, within the retail banking business at Société Générale, succinctly commented:

Financial institutions that are successful at delivering service quality will benefit through greater customer loyalty and wallet share, and by getting the customer relationship on to a complete, lifetime basis. . . . Service is the key to differentiation.[9]

On a slightly lighter note, consider for a moment the rather unusual lengths that some U.S. retail financial services organizations are currently going to, to attract and retain customers:

On US high streets, the biggest demand for premises is not from new coffee shops but from banks opening branches. Resembling their UK counterparts, US banks are becoming more customer focused and increasingly are looking to retailers for ideas on how to build a better bank branch.

US banks believe there is a direct relationship between the time spent in a store and the average amount that a consumer spends. They have found that a better branch brings in more customers who do more business.

Now some US banks greet customers with coffee: Wells Fargo and Bank of America have signed contracts with Starbucks to operate shops inside selected branches. Oregon-based Umpqua Bank started serving coffee—the company's own blend—in its branches in 1996.

US banks also look at the exact placement of their teller counters and monitor customers' reactions to their every move.

Bank of America looked to The Walt Disney Company for inspiration on how to interact with customers. The bank made a distinction between "on stage" (facing customers) and "off stage" (on breaks). When on stage, Bank of America branch workers are asked to smile and wear their name tags. Off stage, they are free to let down their guards.

Bank of America also liked how Sephora, the cosmetics retailer, removed most of the physical barriers between its sales staff and its customers. In the bank's new branches, the strategy is to set up more interactions where the teller stands next to the customer, rather than interacting across a counter.

Washington Mutual, meanwhile, has a play area for children with an activity table, books, Gameboys and more. The section features a big-screen TV playing children's videos, and other screens beckon children with Nintendo and PlayStation games.[10]

We opened this section by asking why the need to continually satisfy customers is driving the business process excellence agenda in many organizations today. The answer is simple. Customers are becoming increasingly value-savvy. If your organization doesn't continually meet customers' needs through delivering products and services in accordance with their requirements, your customers may find a financial services organization that can and will.

A marketplace war is raging for *customer loyalty*. The war is being fought one customer at a time. The war will further intensify over time. The prize is worth fighting for, but once achieved can easily be lost, rarely to be regained. Achieving *customer satisfaction* is the key to winning the war for *customer loyalty* and is a nonnegotiable requirement for financial services organizations that are truly committed to creating sustainable value for their shareholders. Business Process Excellence offers the methods, tools, and techniques to enable organizations to better understand and meet their customers' ever-changing requirements.

Key Driver #2: The Need to Create Sustainable Shareholder Value

To continue our earlier example for a moment: if we were shareholders at Abbey, we wouldn't be too pleased about having to hand over GBP800,000 of our net profits to the Financial Services Authority as a fine. If the organization were using a Six Sigma approach, it would refer to this figure as a Cost of Poor Quality (COPQ). In truth, this is just the direct cost; there are also many indirect financial impacts, such as loss in profit from lost customers and lost revenue associated with the potential inability to acquire new customers—and these typically are much harder to quantify.

In fact, identifying *defects* and *waste* in a service and transactional environment is often very difficult and poses a significant challenge in quantifying and targeting improvement efforts. Here are the key reasons why we believe this is the case:

- *The end product is less tangible.* It's often information, money, or an experience.
- *The process is less visible.* Typically, an employee working on a manufacturing assembly line is able to see the physical process that the product goes through on its way to becoming finished goods. In a financial services environment, the process is much less visible. For example, a telephone call center representative may be presented with a call. The representative may access some information on a computer screen to address the call and then hit the "enter" key, and

whoosh, the information is gone! The representative typically has very little idea of where the transaction subsequently goes and what happens to it next.

- *Waste and defects are less visible.* How do you identify waste in a telephone call center? Within a manufacturing environment, it's often swept up at the end of each shift, in front of everyone!
- *The distance between the root cause of the defect and its place of discovery is often greater.* A data entry error may not be discovered for many months, and then it becomes extremely frustrating for the customer to reconcile his or her account and for all concerned to recreate what had occurred that caused the problem in the first place.
- *Performance data are not so readily available.* Service processes are commonly not well measured, and available data are often tied up in IT systems, from where it's generally challenging to distill meaningful operational information.

The good news is that Six Sigma and Lean offer organizations a number of tools and techniques to identify, reduce, and, in some cases, totally eliminate defects and waste.

At one leading U.S.-based financial services organization, the process improvement team established a very strong focus on *rework* as a basis for "Driving Innovation through the Six Sigma Lens." The organization defined rework as "any effort that must be done again because the original work was ineffective, incomplete, incorrect or lost."[11] What's particularly interesting is that the organization has identified a set of examples that are specific to the nature of its work within financial services:

Repair/Reprocess

- Rekey customer information.
- Redirect funds into the correct account.
- Rescan images.

Rehandle

- Locate items that need to be reprocessed.
- Return misrouted items to the correct area.
- Repackage work that was previously processed.

Recheck

- Verify that work was processed correctly.

Reanalyze

- Repull data to verify that accounts are balanced.
- Recalculate data to verify that corrections were made.

Retrain

- Reexplain procedures to associates.
- Reemphasize policies to associates.
- Reiterate acceptable work standards.

As you review the above list, you might ask yourself whether you know the costs of these *rework* activities in your organization—or even for your own department. In our experience, these costs are rarely measured within financial services organizations to the extent they should be. Consequently, it's not surprising that many organizations are failing to optimize shareholder value creation, as they carry a lot of unnecessary rework-related costs in their operations without knowing it.

As shareholders of such an organization, we wouldn't be too happy with that situation—and neither should you tolerate it! In fact, the implications of not understanding the fully loaded "end-to-end" costs, defects, waste, and all, of delivering products and services in the market are considerable:

> *In a world of end-to-end, customer-focused processes, what matters in the marketplace is the cost of entire processes, regardless of who owns which part of the chain. Tracking this cost requires end-to-end visibility and value management. Cost advantages are the way newcomers enter and dominate mature markets. Almost always, these newcomers succeed by bundling superior processes and associated technologies to form a new "killer value chain."*
>
> *As Peter Drucker notes in* Management Challenges of the 21st Century: *"Executives need to organize and manage, not only the cost chain, but also everything else—including strategy and product planning—as one economic whole, regardless of the legal boundaries of individual companies.*

This is the shift from cost-led pricing to price-led costing." The very same point can be applied to outsourcing, alliances and joint ventures.

Companies with a BPM capability will be able to serve their customers better and faster. They will be able to offer higher quality at a lower cost with greater economies of scale, increasing their profitability. They will be able to respond to new marketplace opportunities more readily by bundling or unbundling business relationships in both demand and supply channels.[12]

Interestingly, in a survey jointly conducted by Pricewaterhouse-Coopers and the Economist Intelligence Unit in 2004, significant gaps were identified between the goals, actions, and resulting benefits achieved at financial services institutions around the world. The survey—conducted with 227 financial services executives from Canada, the United States, Europe, and Asia—examined the top issues that financial institutions face with regard to improving performance.

Fifty-three percent of the institutions surveyed identified customer service as one of their top three competitive advantages followed by 49 percent selecting sales, branding and marketing and 38 percent who opt for quality and performance of actual products and services. However, very few financial institutions said that they were satisfied with their performance in these areas.

Curiously, although rising customer expectations were indicated as being one of the main factors that drive performance improvement initiatives, many more respondents (63 percent) prioritize these initiatives on the basis of opportunities to improve profitability than on the impact to customer service (34 percent).[13]

To our minds, this last paragraph is particularly revealing about the inherent lack of understanding of the relationship between customer satisfaction and profitability that seems to permeate the financial services industry today.

Increasingly, however, there's evidence that even the hard-nosed, value-savvy equity research analysts acknowledge and understand the value that Six Sigma can create for organizations. In June 2004, Morgan Stanley Equity Research analysts Scott Soler and John Kiani published a research paper on Dominion Resources,[14] an organization operating in the electric utilities sector. In the paper, Soler and Kiani remarked: "The company currently has 300 active Six Sigma projects, which management believes will increase Dominion's profitability by $20 to $30 million per year in 2004 and 2005." And, not surprisingly, they subsequently commented: "Dominion's management team ranks in the top quartile of management teams in the North American electric and gas utilities, in our view."

Incidentally, this faith appears to have been well placed. In its "2004 Annual Letter to Shareholders," Dominion senior executives noted that, "The team likes a challenge. It easily beat [the] ambitious goal, racking up nearly $100 million in hard savings!"

Quite simply, failing to satisfy customers' requirements undoubtedly impacts profitability, and yet an argument that is often made by improvement agnostics is that if we satisfied all of our customers' requirements, we wouldn't make any money. Approaches such as Six Sigma and Lean provide the methods, tools, and techniques to enable organizations to solve this paradox. And there are numerous project examples where financial services organizations have used such approaches to simultaneously increase value for both customers *and* shareholders. For example, eliminating non-value-adding steps in a process is likely to reduce both the cycle time of the process and the associated cost of the process. We'll discuss some of these project examples further in Chapter 12.

GE (Capital) is an excellent example of an early-adopter organization that really figured the customer-shareholder value relationship out. On the basis of this understanding, the company positioned its Six Sigma approach as the way in which it could "satisfy customers' needs profitably." This positioning seems to be favored by a number of "fast-follower" financial services organizations that have subsequently adopted and adapted this statement for their own purposes.

Later in this section we'll outline some real-life Six Sigma implementation success stories from leading financial services organizations that have generated billions of dollars of value for their shareholders. For now, let's move onto the third key driver of business process excellence—the need to comply with regulatory requirements.

Key Driver #3: The Need to Comply with Regulatory Requirements

The financial services industry today is, for the most part, a highly regulated environment. With the need to comply with an increasing number of regulatory requirements such as Sarbanes Oxley (SOX), Gramm-Leach-Bliley, and Basel II, together with a plethora of anti–money-laundering legislation (especially in Europe), financial services organizations are increasingly realizing the importance of business process management methods as a means to achieve compliance.

Let's take SOX as a case in point. Section 404 (effective in 2004) requires an organization's annual 10K report[15] to contain:

a. Management's statement of responsibility for establishing and maintaining an adequate internal control structure and procedures for financial reporting
b. Management's assessment of the effectiveness of the internal control structure and procedures for financial reporting
c. External auditor's attestation to management's assessment

As a result, organizations must document information about their internal controls in order for their external auditors to be able to validate management's statements of compliance effectiveness. This is driving organizations to establish a continuous and efficient certification process, and many organizations are now using a business process management approach that enables them to understand the transaction trail as a process and as the basis for establishing appropriate controls at appropriate points.

The underlying needs of this new legislation are to improve performance, the key aspects of which are visibility, transparency, and the provision of reliable, credible information. In a study conducted by the Business Process Management Forum[16] of 230 cross-industry members in 2004, 73 percent of respondents indicated that they're concerned about processes, tools, and methodologies used to track performance as a result of Sarbanes-Oxley.

Interestingly, at a broader level, the survey also reflected a profound awareness of the need for business process management, with 95 percent of respondents saying they are somewhat or extremely sensitized to the need for better business process management.

The cost of noncompliance is well documented with some high-profile cases recently—including the case of Abbey, reported earlier. However, the operational cost of compliance is an increasing burden for many organizations, especially smaller banks. In general, smaller banks often face a disproportionate pressure in their efforts to meet compliance requirements because these financial institutions, active in products such as mortgages, home equity loans, or other personal loans, have lending processes that involve a mixture of semiautomated business processes, paper documents, and multiple manual steps.

Increasingly, financial services organizations are leveraging their business process excellence efforts such as Six Sigma, Lean, and in particular BPM approaches—with their focus on business process documentation, performance measurement, and controls—to enable and assist their regulatory compliance activities.

In fact, following on from Y2K efforts, a number of organizations are now beginning to use an approach based on the concept of a common operational platform (COP)—essentially a commonly held view, throughout an organization, of the organization's processes—to facilitate the delivery, not only of regulatory compliance, but also process improvement, performance management, outsourcing, technology architecture, and business continuity. And with the advent of sophisticated process software tools, this approach to establishing a process-based common operational platform seems set to continue.

Key Driver #4: The Need to Address Scale and Complexity

Scale, achieved through consolidation and rationalization, is a key operating theme within the global financial services industry today. In fact, many commentators hold the view that the continuing consolidation in the industry will eventually lead to only a handful of players emerging as the super-majors—organizations such as Citigroup and HSBC may well be among the contenders today.

Part of the basis for this perspective is the commonly held view that transaction processing in the financial services industry is a scale-based game—the organization with the most transactions wins! This is obviously only one factor for sustainable business success, but scale is no doubt very important.

First Data Corporation (FDC) is an excellent example of how a third-party provider can become a market leader through an unbeatable cost of service. FDC is a leader in payment solutions, and its customers include government agencies, financial institutions, retailers, and consumers. Today, it's the industry leader in the global credit card processing arena. The organization initially built up its market share by offering credit card processing to small financial  institutions in the United States that lacked the means to do it themselves. This enabled FDC to acquire operating scale and processing knowledge before expanding into the more complex (multicurrency) international markets.

In its 2002 annual report, FDC described its commitment to Six Sigma and what it was looking to achieve from its introduction:

> *First Data is committed to being a learning organization, employing Six Sigma techniques to constantly improve and enhance the company's structures, its technology and business processes, and the talent and abilities inherent in its 29,000 employees. The focus of all this progressive energy is, of course, to satisfy our customers, sharpen our competitive advantages and make the entire organization smarter, more agile and capable of sustaining its position as the industry leader.*

Today, in an increasingly larger and more complex operating environment, FDC continues to be committed to Six Sigma, and as described on its internal Web site, determined to excel by focusing on its entire end-to-end processes:

> *Six Sigma provides tools for First Data to measure our current performance and improve in areas where we can do better. By working on bettering entire processes, not just parts and pieces, we'll experience significant breakthroughs in improving our performance. First Data constantly strives to increase growth, productivity and revenue while reducing expenses along the way. By improving our ability to deliver what customers value, we'll increase their satisfaction and ensure every client remains loyal to, and recommends, First Data.*

In 2002 the IBM Institute for Value Management[17] observed that cross-border equity trading volumes had been rising significantly. In fact, U.S. dollar volumes in and out of the United States tripled between 1990 and 1995, from US$615 billion to US$1.7 trillion. Furthermore, cross-border trades in 2000 totaled US$10.6 trillion, over six times the amount traded in 1995.

Scale is often accompanied by complexity, and with complexity there are consequences. In 2002, the Global Straight Through Processing Association (GSTPA) estimated that 15 percent of all cross-border trades failed to settle on time. Estimates from the Society for Worldwide Interbank Financial Telecommunication (SWIFT) were even higher. SWIFT suggested that on-time settlement lag between the foreign exchange and the equity transaction makes hedging risk difficult, particularly when considering the significant amounts involved.

In fact, the growth in the number of products offered and geographies served has led to a complex and inefficient collateral and liquidity management process. Firms often interact with a large number of correspondent banks, as well as numerous clearing and settlement providers.

The IBM analysis explains that complexity has made it increasingly difficult for organizations to have a transparent near real-time view of collateral on a global basis. Lacking this view, organizations operating in the financial markets are unable to optimize their asset utilization, and the cost of managing exceptions is high. Connecting and automating collateral and liquidity management processes through Straight-Through Processing (i.e., end-to-end processing) can help firms achieve significant cost savings.

Six Sigma offers organizations a very powerful way of viewing the true efficiency of processes that cut across many different functional areas and many different entities. The approach used is called Rolled Throughput Yield. It sounds a bit complicated, but really it's quite simple and similar to the concept of Straight-Through Processing.

In the generic financial services example shown in Figure 2.2, the yield—the percentage of good products and services produced (i.e., without defects)—is shown for each step of the process. By multiplying

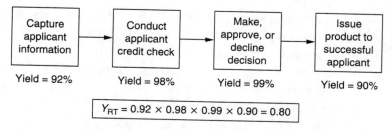

Figure 2.2 Rolled throughput yield.
The quality of an end-to-end process is generally lower than the quality of each step in the process.

the yield numbers together, we reach a rolled throughput yield (YRT) of 0.80 (i.e., 80 percent). This means that only 80 percent of transactions will be delivered without a single defect. In other words, there's a 20 percent probability that a transaction will encounter a defect as it's processed!

Bank of America

Another example of scale and complexity comes from Bank of America. Consider the summary of the number of potential customer "touch points" and the volume of customer contacts at Bank of America shown in Box 2.1.[18]

At a total of 5.4 billion transactions in 2003, this is equivalent to over 170 customer contacts a second! That figure represents millions upon millions of service interactions each day. Such a scale of business offers

Box 2.1

Customer Touch Point	Annual Volume of Transactions
Debit and credit card transactions	2,100 million
ATMs (16,000)	925 million
Banking centers (5,700)	900 million
Online services	800 million
Call centers	700 million
Total transactions	5,425 million

Note: Excludes 2,500 mortgage applications processed per day.
Source: Bank of America

the organization a great opportunity to both get it right, and get it wrong for its customers.

Another interesting scale example is in the area of ATMs. Despite its limited service offerings, the ATM is now the most commonly used customer touch point for most retail banks, with over 1.3 million machines in operation worldwide in 2003. For now, it remains a trusted and familiar device on which many customers depend.

Recent research[19] shows that the global ATM market will continue growing to 1.7 million by 2009 (see Figure 2.3) and confirms that ATMs and cash dispensers have become the most important customer service channel for retail banks in terms of frequency of customer interactions. Over 56 billion transactions were carried out at ATMs in 2003. While most of these were cash withdrawals, the number and share of noncash transactions, such as cell phone top-ups, balance inquiries, and cash and check deposits, are growing.

Increasingly, the branch is enjoying a resurgence with new self-service machines for cash withdrawal, deposits, and account information (such as mini-statements). And new card technologies, driven largely by chip-card payment technology mandated by EMV (Master-Card, Visa, Europay), mean that the ATM could provide an array of as-yet unexplored, custom-tailored services to customers, further adding to processing complexity.

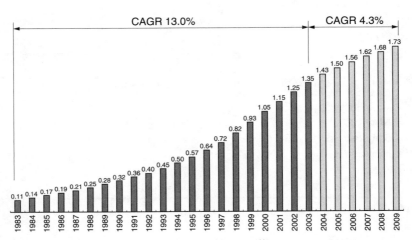

Figure 2.3 Global ATM installations (in millions), 1983–2009.

Source: Global ATM Market and Forecasts to 2009 (Retail Banking Research)

Such scale and associated complexity requires extremely robust business processes.

Lloyds TSB, with 15 million customers, about 71,000 employees and, by market capitalization, the U.K.'s fifth largest financial services organization, has an excellent appreciation of scale and associated complexity. Its operational processes **You first** 🐎 Lloyds TSB need to address the requirements of multiple customer segments, through multiple channels, with a multiple product mix (see Figure 2.4).[20] Given this complexity, it's no wonder that Lloyds TSB is one of the leading exponents of process management. We'll describe Lloyds TSB's approach further in Chapter 11.

Conversely, however, complexity, if managed, also offers new business opportunities. Today, Capital One is a broadly diversified financial services company with operations in the United States, the United Kingdom, and Canada. Capital **CapitalOne** | what's in your wallet?" One offers a wide variety of financial services, including credit cards, auto loans, small business loans, home equity loans, installment loans, and deposit and savings products. With more than 50 million customer accounts, one of the most recognized brands

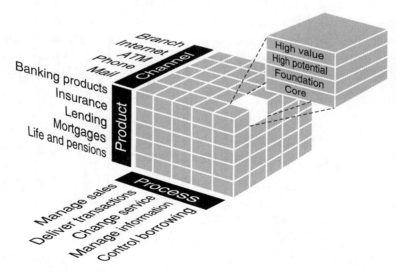

Figure 2.4 Process, product and channel complexity
Source: Lloyds TSB

in the United States, and more than 300 locations throughout Louisiana and Texas, Capital One is one of the largest customer franchises in North America.

It successfully utilizes its proprietary databases containing consumer credit information to operate a set of complex algorithms to assess risk. On the basis of this analysis, the organization is able to offer operationally risk-adjusted products at appropriate pricing to customers across the credit spectrum.

Closing Thoughts on Scale and Complexity

The need to address scale and complexity is a key driving force of change that places unprecedented demands on an organization's operational processes. Six Sigma's focus on customers, processes, and facts and data, coupled with Lean's focus on value and waste elimination, provide powerful means to address these challenges.

As you will see later in a case study about a Eurocountry bank, business process excellence approaches such as Six Sigma and Lean not only enable organizations to reduce costs, but can also create operational capacity and the scalability to address business growth requirements.

By establishing and maintaining an end-to-end core process perspective, financial services organizations can focus on what truly creates value for their customers as their businesses scale up and become ever more complex. This is particularly important in a global marketplace where organizations need to increasingly manage their operations across an *extended enterprise.*

Key Driver #5: The Need to Operate across an Extended Enterprise

In recent years, Business Process Outsourcing (BPO) and offshoring have become increasingly favored operational models by many financial services organizations. In this section we'll explore what they are, the emerging trends and challenges they present, and why organizations are increasingly utilizing leading business process excellence methods, tools, and techniques to improve the management of their outsourced and offshored business processes.

Essentially five different types of activities fall under the general label of business process outsourcing. Following are the key definitions[21] for each of these.

Business process outsourcing involves first examining the processes that comprise the business and its functional units and then working with focused service providers to both reengineer and outsource these at the same time. BPO involves the full transfer of responsibility for functions such as transaction processing, policy servicing, claims management, HR, finance, and compliance to the outsourcing company. The outsourcing provider then administers these functions in its own systems to agreed service standards and at a guaranteed cost. Some of the BPO contracts call for performance-based payouts, tying vendor payments to business performance or overall cost savings.

Business process offshoring is the transfer of business tasks (e.g., case setup) or business processes (e.g., call centers) to a low-cost country such as India, China, or the Philippines. The interaction is conducted over telecom networks and the Internet. Offshoring typically includes tasks like transaction or accounts processing, credit card processing, call centers, translation, and transcription. Most of this work can be sent without the need for in-person interaction. The offshoring of support functions is still relatively new. The offshoring wave began with IT/software services in the 1980s and accelerated in the 1990s with the Y2K hysteria. With the global economic slowdown, offshoring has vaulted to the forefront as an effective cost-cutting technique that takes advantage of labor price differentials and favorable skill-performance ratios.

Business transformation outsourcing (BTO) is a natural extension of the more tactical BPO model and involves the transfer of responsibility for all back-office functions, as well as a comprehensive business change management process, to an external vendor. The objective is to maximize the long-term benefits of the BPO operations, resulting in a comprehensive business transformation (or overhaul). Transformation outsourcing is not a tactical issue but a forward-looking strategic tool for change. The logic: big gains in performance come about only through business transformation.

Multisourcing is the management and distribution of different business processes among multiple BPO vendors. For instance, HR processes are outsourced to one best-of-breed vendor, logistics to another, IT development and maintenance to another. Risk mitigation is a primary driver behind multisourcing. One aspect of multisourcing is to use multiple suppliers to eliminate lock-in and achieve so-called best-of-breed advantages. This is especially true for U.S. and European firms, which often like to spread offshore development to a variety of vendors and locations. Multisourcing also covers the different delivery models. These include:

- *Onshoring*—outsourcing to another company within the home market
- *Near-shoring*—for a U.S.-based company, outsourcing typically to Mexico or Canada
- *Offshoring*—outsourcing to another country such as Ireland or India

Shared services, a form of "internal outsourcing," enables organizations to achieve economies of scale by creating a separate internal entity within the company to perform specific services, such as payroll, accounts payable, travel, and expense processing. A typical shared-services initiative takes advantage of enterprise applications and other technological developments, enabling the company to achieve further improvements to quality in processes such as finance, accounting, procurement, IT, and human resources. At the core of shared services is the idea that new technologies offer businesses the opportunity to (1) make better use of scarce skills, (2) provide information and services more efficiently, and (3) reduce the cost of administration.

Having provided these different definitions, we shall—at the risk of confusing you—simply use BPO as a general term to reference any of the above approaches.

As we described earlier, the overall BPO market has been significantly increasing in recent years. This is especially so across the financial services industry as organizations look to reduce their operating costs. Consider this report summary from NelsonHall,[22] a global BPO analyst firm, which announced that the value of international BPO contract awards in the first nine months of 2004 reached $18.6 billion, a 44 percent increase over the same period the previous year!

- HR outsourcing and financial services–specific BPO remain key growth opportunities in both the United States and Europe, but whereas finance and accounting outsourcing has shown some growth in North America, the expansion in this sector in Europe has not been significant.

- Despite the continuing importance of the life insurance sector in the European financial services industry, the banking sector is again showing the greatest growth and accounted for 65 percent of the contract value awarded in the last year.
- Front- and middle-office processes are still dominating BPO contract awards (76 percent), with back-office support services making up only 24 percent of contract activity over the past 12 months.

Let's now take a look at some recent outsourcing news regarding two high-profile European-based global financial institutions.

HSBC is one of the largest banking and financial services organizations in the world, with an international network comprising over 9,800 offices in 77 countries and territories covering Europe, the Asia-Pacific region, the Americas, the Middle East, and Africa. In early 2005, HSBC announced its decision to double its offshore back-office staff to 25,000 as part of a four-year program it started in 2003 to cut more than $1 billion of its costs.[23] At the time this decision was announced, HSBC already had about 13,000 staff across 10 offshore centers in Asia, handling functions such as telephone support for customers in Europe and the United States. With its decision to double its offshore back-office staff, it will expand to as many as 15 centers over the next three years.

The bank had already announced 4,500 job cuts in the United Kingdom by 2006 as a result of offshoring, and half of these had already been made. Outside the United Kingdom, HSBC is creating 500 jobs a month in its offshore service centers across Asia.

The news was not well received by a number of HSBC employees in the United Kingdom, who formed picket lines outside of some branches and outside the company's annual meeting to protest at HSBC's policy of offshoring jobs. The workers claimed that customers had been choosing to come into branches rather than deal with the bank's global call centers, adding more work for the branch staff. The bank denied there was anything wrong.

The cost-reduction argument is compelling. According to HSBC, it saves about $20,000 for every job moved offshore. Incidentally, HSBC has recently established its global Six Sigma Center of Excellence in India.

ABN Amro, a prominent international bank with over 3,000 branches in more than 60 countries, a staff of about 96,000 full-time equivalents, and total assets of over €880 billion as of December 31, 2005, announced in September 2005 that it had signed contracts with five different vendors to outsource €1.8 billion of IT services.[24] The initiative is expected to provide savings of €258 million per year beginning in 2007. Combined with other reengineering efforts in offshoring, real estate, and human resources, annual savings should reach €750 million as of 2008.

ABN·AMRO

Large components of ABN Amro's back office have already been offshored to sites in India. This further outsourcing news will involve the shedding of about 3,200 of its 5,000 IT employees worldwide, with about 2,000 of those moving to the selected vendors:

- IBM will provide the management of ABN Amro's worldwide IT infrastructure, including servers, storage systems, and desktops.
- Tata Consultancy Services (TCS) will provide support and enhancement for selected business units.
- Infosys Technologies will provide application support and enhancement for selected business units.
- Accenture, IBM, TCS, Infosys, and Patni Computer Systems will provide application development across all business units.

In addition to cost savings, ABN Amro expects the initiative to provide it with "better and earlier access to newer technology," according to Hugh Scott-Barrett, the chief operating officer.

In 2003, a report on outsourcing in *BAI Banking Strategies*[25] suggested that banks were becoming increasingly selective in their outsourcing activities. At that time, Bank of America was spending about $7 billion annually with outsource vendors, about 80 percent of which was spent with 280 suppliers, many of them branch-related.

Interestingly, Bank of America now ensures that it holds the reins, especially when it comes to measuring performance, so much so that the organization requires its largest suppliers to become certified in Six Sigma, in a training course adapted and taught by the bank.

Although the financial benefits of pursuing a BPO strategy are relatively clear, the challenges that financial services organizations face in successfully executing such a strategy are, in many cases, not fully understood at the outset.

It's highly likely that we'll witness a number of changes in focus and approach over the next three to five years as financial services organizations address a number of operating challenges that are emerging with the BPO model, and with offshoring in particular. Recent issues involve reports that:

- "Indian BPO company employees face psychological issues,"[26] because they are often asked to change their accents and adopt Western names so they can better relate to customers
- The U.S. Office of the Comptroller of the Currency (OCC) will investigate offshoring operations.[27] Previously the OCC depended on U.S. banks' internal operations to monitor the security of their offshore captive sites or third-party provider contracts, primarily in India, but it is now taking a closer look itself at the foreign operations. The policy change comes in the aftermath of a major theft involving employees of an Indian business process outsourcer.
- Nasscom, India's software industry lobbying group, is pushing for more privacy protection and standards[28] and has outlined a plan for stricter privacy protection laws. The plan calls for more self-regulation within companies, more education, and a greater awareness of security concerns and higher standards for encrypting sensitive information. The group also wants to emphasize compliance with international standards and bring best practices to India. India already has an information technology privacy act, but there is no industrywide system for checking employee backgrounds.

In fact, there have been a small number of high-profile outsourcing reversals recently. One notable example is JPMorgan Chase's decision to bring its Card Services Plastic and Statement Processing in-house. The internal processing capability **JPMorganChase** available at its processing facility (shown in Figure 2.5) in Columbus, Ohio, enables it to achieve a minimum of $17 million

Figure 2.5 JPMorgan Chase processing facility.

in cost savings per year and in addition offers quality and timeliness advantages over an outsourced process.[29]

You may be asking yourself what all this has to do with Lean, Six Sigma, or any other approach to achieving business process excellence. Our view is that these fundamental changes to the way in which financial services organizations operate create significant coordination, alignment, and management challenges across the end-to-end processes that their customers experience. These relatively newly created extended enterprises and supply chains cut across multiple organizational functions, third-party partners, and suppliers, in many cases operating across different cultures, locations, time zones, and geographies. These organizations require a highly structured business process management approach in place to ensure they can continue to satisfy customers' requirements while reaping the obvious short-term financial benefits that such operating models can provide to their shareholders. Shipping a bad process overseas may reduce costs in the short term but rarely changes the process itself; thus the organization still has a bad process, the customer still does not understand what to do, and customer frustration is often compounded. At a minimum, organizations considering BPO should institute a process measurement system that tracks the critical quality dimensions for the processes being moved, and enables improvements to be made effectively.

Key Driver #6: The Need to Leverage Enabling and Accelerating Technology

Much of what we've described so far is highly dependent upon technology. Not only is technology enabling ever-increasing volumes of transactions to be processed faster and cheaper on a unit cost basis, but it's also accelerating and reshaping the whole customer experience. Consider, for example, the availability and exponential increase in the use of phone and Internet channels by retail banking customers who, just 10 years ago, were able to conduct their transactions only at branches or at ATMs.

In his 1999 book, *Business @ the Speed of Thought,* Bill Gates reiterated this same concept:

> *Today bank information systems have to do more than manage huge amounts of financial data. They have to put more intelligence about customers into the hands of business strategists and loan officers. They have to enable customers to securely access information and pay bills online while the bank's knowledge workers collaborate on higher-value activities.*[30]

While one could argue about the amount of benefit consumers have derived since these comments were made, there is no denying the continuing potential for significant growth in this area.

Over recent years, IT priorities in financial services organizations appear to have shifted from long-term, discretionary projects aimed at improving customer service to more strategic efforts geared toward lowering costs. At the same time, IT organizations have been coping with the new regulatory emphasis on mitigating operational risk in response to global political realities.

As with business process transformation and improvement efforts, many of these efforts were, and continue to be, hampered by business processes that have evolved around vertically integrated functional areas, each with its own associated systems, and more often than not, isolated silos of data. More recently, IT organizations have been increasingly looking to merge these disparate systems across organizations and integrate application portfolios to reduce costs, better manage risk, and enable the organization to present a unified face to its customers.

As financial services organizations increasingly focus on using business process excellence methods such as Six Sigma and Lean to transform and improve their business processes, they are creating significant demand for IT changes. For the IT organization this means that its capabilities—people, applications, methods, and infrastructure—must align even more closely with the operational strategies and priorities of the business. This alignment has fundamental implications on spending decisions, such as which systems to maintain or enhance and which to reengineer or replace.

As all banks typically offer essentially the same products and services, those that take a more holistic view of the customer and provide a consistent customer experience across channels have a great competitive advantage. They can get deeper into the relationship with the customer—and deeper into the customer's wallet. The leading financial services organizations are getting very good at cross-channel management governance.

For example, at one of the largest U.S. commercial banking organizations with total assets approaching $180 billion, the director of e-business chairs a monthly meeting with representatives from all the lines-of-business and key functional areas such as the Enterprise Information Services technology group. Representatives from the support areas of branch banking and the call center are also included. The goal is to review and confirm e-business project priorities across the company.

Whether a regional retail bank or a global investment firm, an integrated view of the customer is critical to sustained growth. This customer-centric emphasis will drive purposeful IT projects that are well aligned with business strategy. However, all too often, it's an organization's systems that seem to dictate its processes, and the products and services that are offered and delivered to its customers (see Figure 2.6). We call this the "IT stranglehold"— in truth, it's *not* the Six Sigma way.

While it's indisputable that technology will have an ever-increasing impact on the way in which customers interact with financial services organizations, it's also critically important to remember that technology is simply an enabler and accelerator of business processes:

> *Process management heralds a renaissance in process thinking and process-centered organizational design. And this renaissance is not being driven by technological innovation alone. Far from it. The principal drivers are economic. Business processes, not applications or databases, are the highest value assets in business today, but the value of those assets lies not only in their execution, but an ability to manage them.*[31]

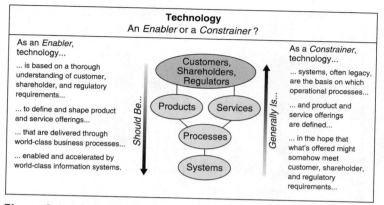

Figure 2.6 Is your organization a victim of the IT stranglehold?

Those financial services organizations that are able to most effectively align and prioritize their business improvement and technology activities within an integrated portfolio of opportunities stand to gain the most from technology enablement and acceleration.

Closing Comments

In our view, the key driving forces of change (see Figure 2.7) that we've described in this chapter—the need for financial services organizations to continually satisfy customers, create sustainable shareholder value, comply with regulatory requirements, address scale and complexity, operate across an extended enterprise, and leverage enabling and accelerating technology—require organizations to radically rethink how they deliver products and services to their customers.

We believe that *Business Process Excellence*—an approach that links the very best of Business Process Management, Lean, Six Sigma, Kaizen, and other methods, tools, and techniques to achieve improved business performance—is a fundamental requirement for the success of financial services organizations today and increasingly in the future.

Perhaps we should let Michael Hammer have the last word on this topic for now. In closing his white paper "Business Processes in Financial Services,"[32] he wrote:

Business process management, measurement, and re-design is taking center stage in modern management. The opportunities for performance improvement that processes offer are simply too great to be ignored, and financial services organizations can no longer let this opportunity pass. The payoffs are enormous, the need is pressing, and the enabling technology is in place. The time to begin is now.

Key Driving Forces of Change

Financial services organizations have to

1. Continually satisfy customers
2. Create sustainable shareholder value
3. Comply with regulatory requirements
4. Address scale and complexity
5. Operate across an extended enterprise
6. Leverage enabling and accelerating technology

Figure 2.7
Copyright Hayler and Nichols 2006

Notes

1. We will address employee-, ethical-, and societal-related themes throughout the book.
2. Based on a real-life incident, although names and account details have been changed to protect confidentiality.
3. Lisa Ducharme, Customer Experience Director, "Strategically Capturing the Customer Experience," IQPC Six Sigma for Financial Services Conference (July 27, 2004), New York.
4. Data are from independent studies conducted with customers who transact in Wachovia's financial centers. Scores prior to 1Q02 are for legacy First Union only. Scores are based on a scale of 1 (low) to 7 (high).
5. Data are from independent studies conducted with customers who transact in Wachovia's financial centers. The definition of a loyal customer is a customer who gives a rating of 7, based on a scale of 1 (low) to 7 (high), on all three loyalty questions (satisfaction with Wachovia, likelihood to recommend, and likelihood to repurchase).
6. Ken Thompson, Citigroup Financial Services Conference (February 1, 2006).
7. "Simplify to Succeed. Optimize the Customer Franchise and Achieve Operational Scale: Retail Financial Institutions in 2005," IBM Business Consulting Services (2002).

8. In Six Sigma this surge, driven by the flood of endowment complaints in relation to a specific and unique set of circumstances, would be considered "special cause" variation. It's not representative of the "common" levels of variation typically seen in the process.

9. "Simplify to Succeed." See note 7.

10. Jane Croft, "Time to Wake Up and Smell the Coffee," *London Financial Times* (April 5, 2005).

11. Greg Swindell, Senior Vice President, Wachovia, July 2004.

12. Howard Smith and Peter Fingar, *Business Process Management: The Third Wave* (Tampa, FL: Meghan-Kiffer Press, 2002).

13. PricewaterhouseCoopers, "Global Financial Services Face Challenges to Improve Performance," Toronto, December 16, 2004.

14. Scott Soler and John Kiani, "Is the Sum > Than the Parts?" Morgan Stanley Equity Research (June 2, 2004).

15. A 10-K report is the audited annual report that most reporting companies file with the Securities and Exchange Commission. It provides a comprehensive overview of the registrant's business. The report must be filed within 90 days after the end of the company's fiscal year (www.ventureline.com/glossary).

16. As reported in www.SearchCIO.com (January 2004).

17. Daniel Latimore, Ian Watson, and Greg Robinson, "Restructuring Costs Rationally for Longer Term Competitiveness in Financial Markets," IBM Institute for Value Management, © IBM Corporation (2002).

18. Presentation by Joe Valasquez, former Bank of America Senior Vice President–Quality & Productivity, "Growing America's Premier Financial Services Company."

19. Published by Retail Banking Research (RBR), a strategic research and consulting firm with close to three decades of experience in retail banking, banking automation, and payment systems.

20. Guy Noble, "Business Process Management and Six Sigma Working Together," Group Service and Sigma Improvement, Lloyds TSB Group.

21. "BPO Terminology: Organizing the Chaos," EBS, a leading technology research and consulting practice specializing in BPO, www.ebstrategy.com.

22. David Bannister, Banking Technology, "Outsourcing Trend Continues Despite High Profile Reversals," NelsonHall (January 2005).

23. Global News Wire–Europe Intelligence Wire (March 2005); *Personnel Today* (May 2005).

24. ABN Amro Press Release (September 2005); *InformationWeek* (September 2005).

25. Elizabeth Judd, "Outsourcing Redefined," *BAI Banking Strategies*, vol. LXXIX, no. 1 (January/February 2003).

26. *The Economic Times* (August 2005).

27. *Bank Technology News* (September 2005).

28. *Financial Times* (May 2005).

29. Chase Card Services Investor Day (February 23, 2005).

30. Bill Gates, *Business @ the Speed of Thought*, (Warner Books, 1999, p. 12).

31. Smith and Fingar, see note 12.

32. Michael Hammer, "Business Processes in Financial Services," Microsoft white paper (September 2003).

Some Success Stories from Leading Financial Services Organizations

L ET'S NOW TAKE A LOOK at some of the financial services organizations that have done just as Michael Hammer suggests,[1] and in so doing, have achieved success from their Six Sigma, Lean, and Business Process Management work.

In fact, at the time of writing, we know of over 50 organizations in the financial services and insurance sectors that utilize Lean and Six Sigma methods, tools, and techniques to improve their business processes. We have listed many of the more notable organizations, according to their industry-sector classification in Box 3.1. We believe there are many more.

The success stories we are about to share are not intended to provide the whole story of who and what these organizations are or where, when, and how they achieved success, but rather to simply outline the various approaches taken and the results achieved so far.

We'll continue to reference successful approaches being taken by these and other organizations throughout the rest of the book. The organizations whose stories we'll outline here are a mixture of early adopters and fast followers. They cover global organizations; financial

Box 3.1

Commercial and Savings Banks	Diversified Financials	Securities	Insurance
• Abbey	• American Express	• Merrill Lynch	• Aetna
• ABN AMRO	• Aon	• Goldman Sachs	• AIG
• Asian Development Bank	• Countrywide Financial	• Charles Schwab	• Allstate
• Bank of America	• GE Capital	• Fidelity	• AXA Insurance
• Bank Negara Indonesia			• Berkshire Hathaway
• Bank Mandiri			• CIGNA
• Barclays			• Consecom
• Capital One Financial			• Jefferson Pilot
• Citigroup			• Lincoln National
• Commonwealth Bank of Australia			• Northwestern Mutual
• Credit Suisse			• Principal Financial
• Development Bank Singapore			• Prudential Financial
• Deutsche Bank			• Unum Provident
• Fifth Third Bancorp			• USAA
• Halifax Bank of Scotland			• Vertex
• Household			• Zurich Financial Services
• HSBC			
• ICICI Bank			
• JPMorgan Chase			
• KeyCorp			
• Lloyds TSB			
• M & S Money			
• Mellon Financial Corp			
• National City Corp			
• Nedcor			
• Overseas Chinese Banking Corporation			
• State Street Bank & Trust Co.			
• UBS			
• Wachovia Corp			
• Washington Mutual			
• Wells Fargo			

services organizations operating in solely the United States, United Kingdom, and Singapore; and different industry sectors. They are:

- Bank of America
- JPMorgan Chase
- American Express
- Countrywide Financial Corporation
- Development Bank of Singapore
- Marks & Spencer Money

Bank of America[2] is the second-largest bank in the United States by assets (behind Citigroup), and it has the most extensive branch network, with more than 5,800 locations. Bank of America continues to grow through selective acquisitions such as FleetBoston in 2004 and, more recently, credit card giant MBNA in early 2006.

Bank of America

Bank of America is one of the most prominent financial services organizations with a corporatewide Six Sigma program, and it is not afraid to talk about its initiative. The scale of the bank's effort coupled with its unique blend of Hoshin[3] planning, Kanri management, and Six Sigma places it at the forefront of financial services organizations striving for business process excellence.

Bank of America began its Six Sigma journey in 2001 as a corporate initiative supported by CEO Ken Lewis, who has been an outstanding senior sponsor of the effort ever since. In our view, one of the most insightful comments that Ken Lewis has made about the bank's Six Sigma efforts, was the following:

There's a whole difference [between] Six Sigma in a manufacturing process and banking. We have found that there are so many processes in our company where . . . looking at it end to end from the client's perspective and solving for the client what they want, we were able to dramatically improve our processes.

This appreciation of the need for looking at the bank's processes "end to end from the client's perspective" is one of the key enablers that has allowed Bank of America to deliver the significant benefits recorded and regularly referenced by Ken Lewis in the bank's Annual Reports to Shareholders.

In the 2003 Annual Report to Shareholders, Lewis reported:

Since launching our Six Sigma efforts less than three years ago, we've saved hundreds of millions of dollars in expenses, cut cycle times in numerous areas of the company by half or more and improved the percentage of customers who rate their satisfaction at 9 or 10 on a 10-point scale from 41% to more than 50%, an increase of almost 2.5 million customers.

In the 2004 Annual Report to Shareholders, he commented on the way in which the bank had successfully utilized Six Sigma methods, tools, and techniques to facilitate the merger transition process of FleetBoston. To our knowledge this is one of the first applications of such an approach to the merger transition process, and according to Ken Lewis's comments, it appears to have delivered considerable value:

The merger transition process [referencing B of A's acquisition of Fleet] itself has been, without qualification, the smoothest and fastest I have seen in my career. From the beginning, we planned and executed the transition and all associated projects with strict adherence to a disciplined Six Sigma approach, improving processes, driving down costs and enhancing quality and productivity along the way.

In fact, Bank of America has expanded its application of Six Sigma even more widely.[4] This point was driven home at the International Society of Six Sigma Practitioners Symposium held in Charlotte, North Carolina, in October 2004. At the symposium, Milton H. Jones, the chief quality and productivity executive, noted:

For the last two years, we've even been requiring that our key vendors use Six Sigma methods, and we're now making sure that they participate in our own Six Sigma training programs.

To date, Six Sigma has helped contribute $2 billion to Bank of America's bottom line since it was implemented, and the bank aims to drive Six Sigma–related savings and revenue gains to $1 billion per year. Over 5,000 of the bank's employees have earned Green Belt, Black Belt, or other Six Sigma certification, which has now become a requisite for many positions at the bank. Interestingly, a growth strategy component at the bank is to "employ Six Sigma process excellence to drive sustainable and differentiated performance and client delight."

The bank's efficiency ratio (noninterest expenses divided by revenue) is a key metric throughout all its business units. As Ken Lewis has stated:

> *If you noticed in the efficiency ratios from our businesses, we have used Six Sigma in every one of them in three or four different places, and we have lowered our operating costs by easily 100 to 200 basis points in those businesses.*

JPMorgan Chase & Co.[5] was built from the successful merger of JPMorgan and Chase Manhattan Bank in December 2000 and the recent merger with Bank One in July 2004.

JPMorganChase ◐   Six Sigma dates back to 1998 at JPMorgan, where it was introduced as a corporatewide initiative focused on expense-reduction projects. Bank One had been using Six Sigma since 2000, where it was introduced in the National Enterprise Operations Group as a business process improvement tool.

Cognizant of how disruptive such initiatives can be to current operations, JPMorgan began applying Six Sigma in selected retail areas such as mortgages, credit cards, and auto finance. This process was then expanded over the next few years to include all the bank's retail and middle-market services.

In 2002, Six Sigma became part of a broader productivity and quality (P&Q) initiative that included Lean, design for Six Sigma (DFSS), activity-based costing, project management, Kaizen, and change leadership.

Six Sigma P&Q became one of JPMorgan Chase's top six strategic initiatives in 2002 and focused not only on expense reduction but on revenue increase and customer satisfaction as well. In its 2002 Annual Report to Shareholders, JPMorgan commented on its Six Sigma approach and the benefits gained:

> *While the market for financial services is far more fragmented on the retail side than it is in wholesale, certain fundamentals apply in both worlds. One is the importance of flawless execution. That is why we are*

*using the Six Sigma approach to drive improvements in quality and effi-
ciency throughout JPMorgan Chase. Whether the product is a $50,000
mortgage or a multibillion-dollar underwriting, we aim to get everything
right the first time.*

Similarly to Bank of America, JPMorgan Chase targeted about $1
billion per year in benefits from its Six Sigma efforts, reporting in its
2002 Annual Report to Shareholders:

*Last year, the firm's clients and shareholders benefited from Six Sigma—
a set of tools that guides teams in understanding what clients need and
then helps them meet those needs flawlessly. Emphasizing customer-focused
operations and rigorous service levels, Six Sigma drove more than $400
million in financial benefits in 2002. Going forward, the launch of Six
Sigma projects is expected to generate benefits of up to $1.0 billion per year.*

In the bank's 2003 Annual Report, William B. Harrison, Jr., the chairman and chief executive officer, wrote in his "Letter to Shareholders":

*In 2003, our productivity and quality efforts yielded more than $1 billion
pre-tax in net financial benefits, more than double those achieved in 2002.
Over one-half of these benefits came from re-engineering key business
processes using the disciplined methodology of Six Sigma.*

Interestingly, the most recent (2004) annual report does not specifically mention Six Sigma, but it does make reference to the bank's continuing commitment to waste reduction and operational efficiency:

*A financial services company cannot win unless it is a low-cost provider.
This requires eliminating waste and creating the most effective systems
and most efficient operations in the business. We are well on our way.*

American Express[6] is a leading organization within
the diversified financials sector. Through its subsidiaries,
American Express provides travel-related, financial
advisory, and international banking services around the
world. The company's products include the American

Express card, the Optima card, and American Express travelers cheque.

American Express began its Six Sigma journey with a pilot initiative in late 1998. A small group of Black Belts across disciplines, functions, and business units were selected and trained and completed their first projects.

After the initial pilot, the program spread slowly to other business units. In early 2000, Six Sigma fell under the leadership of Jim Li, a highly experienced general manager with a strong quality and engineering background, and the effort became more integrated with the corporate strategic initiatives and planning process. This created a step-function improvement in benefits from the company's Six Sigma initiative.

In the 2002 Annual Report to Shareholders, CEO Ken Chenault commented:

> *As part of our reengineering efforts, we have significantly expanded our Six Sigma program across the company. We are using Six Sigma to enhance quality and productivity in key business processes and to eliminate costly errors. In 2002, our Six Sigma activities produced nearly $200 million in financial benefits and delivered important quality enhancements. Since launching Six Sigma at American Express in 1999, we have steadily increased the number of employees trained in Six Sigma tools and principles. In addition to fixing errors within processes, we are also now applying Six Sigma principles to product design and development in order to build quality in from the start. We view Six Sigma as an important element of our ongoing commitment to service quality and to providing our customers with experiences that continually meet and exceed their expectations.*

At the American Express Annual Meeting of Shareholders in April 2003, Ken Chenault explained:

> *The company remains committed to improving our processes and increasing our efficiency, particularly through the use of Six Sigma. Our goal is to deliver $1 billion in margin improvement in 2003, above and beyond the $2 billion plus we've delivered over the last two years.*

Subsequently, as the Six Sigma effort gained traction and became more widely accepted as the means to reengineer its businesses, so the realized benefits significantly increased. In the 2003 Annual Report to Shareholders, Ken Chenault remarked:

Over the past few years, an increasing portion of our reengineering benefits have come from Six Sigma process improvement efforts. In 2003, we significantly expanded Six Sigma training across the company. We are not only using Six Sigma to reduce errors in existing processes, we are also applying it in product development to build quality in from the start. Six Sigma supports both our commitment to quality and to achieving best-in-class economics.

At a presentation to the Lehman Brothers Financial Services Conference in September 2004, executive vice president and chief financial officer Gary Crittenden commented:

We have leveraged and will continue to employ Six Sigma methodologies to achieve ongoing reengineering benefits throughout the organization. In fact, this year, approximately $500 million of the identified reengineering benefits are attributable to our Six Sigma efforts.

More recently, in its 2004 Annual Report, Ken Chenault explains:

We consider reengineering to be a critical and ongoing aspect of our management strategy at American Express. We focus on making core processes more efficient by reducing costs while increasing quality. In fact, much of our savings from reengineering now come from Six Sigma quality improvement projects.

Countrywide Financial[7] is one of the largest independent residential mortgage lending firms in the United States, writing, selling, and servicing prime first mortgages for single-family homes through its Countrywide Homes subsidiary. It also offers home equity loans and subprime mortgages. In addition, Countrywide Financial is a broker-dealer of mortgage-backed

securities; sells property/casualty, health, and credit insurance; and operates Treasury Bank, also known as Countrywide Bank.

In 2001, Countrywide Financial launched its internally developed, proprietary program called *FASTER—flow, analyze, solve, target, execute, and review*. The six-step methodology is modeled after Six Sigma and is specifically designed for the financial services environment. FASTER, as well as the customer satisfaction program *PACE* (proudly achieving customer expectations), is helping Countrywide improve all aspects of its business, from boosting efficiency and enhancing cost-effectiveness to improving customer service.

A year or so into the effort, Countrywide was making good progress—delivering a solid set of results and engaging employees at all levels of the organization. It commented in its 2002 Annual Report to Shareholders:

> *Our passion for excellence was epitomized by the increasing employee utilization of FASTER, a productivity program customized for Countrywide. Similar to Six Sigma used in other industries, FASTER is aimed at making every aspect of our operation better. To date, nearly 5,000 employees have been trained in this discipline. We have over 800 users of FASTER software, and approximately 350 registered FASTER projects under way. The cultural impact has been significant: FASTER has been made accessible to all employees, encouraging a continuous improvement mindset at every level of the Company. In 2002, the first full year of the program, FASTER delivered nearly $11 million in operating profit and identified potential future savings of close to $84 million. Given the high degree of employee buy-in, we expect to see substantially increased results for 2003—including a strong return on investment and thousands more training certifications among our 30,000-person workforce.*

Momentum for the effort continued, and in the 2003 Annual Report to Shareholders the organization was able to report:

> *Since the program's inception in 2001, about 6,000 employees have been trained at various levels of certification, in the FASTER performance management methodology which has resulted in approximately $244 million in productivity gains.*

More recently, progress has continued, and in its 2004 Annual Report to Shareholders, Countrywide Financial noted:

Since the program's inception in 2001, FASTER has delivered $76 million in operating profit and has identified potential future savings of $560 million. Although FASTER continues to benefit the Company financially, the true benefit of the program is cultural—every employee can improve Countrywide's processes, and FASTER gives them the tools and the recognition to do so. At the same time, the PACE group facilitated the gathering of customer service feedback from over 2 million consumers, business partners and employees during 2004.

Our next two real-life success stories are reported in a somewhat different way, and they don't involve the reporting of success in their respective organizations' annual reports as hard financial benefits. In comparison to Bank of America and JPMorgan Chase, these organizations are in the relatively early stages of their journeys. Nevertheless, they have achieved success, albeit in a less quantifiable way, that enables them to continue their respective paths.

The Development Bank of Singapore (DBS)[8] is one of the largest financial services groups in Asia, with almost 5 million customers and operations in 14 markets.

DBS

Given the increasing commoditization of the product offerings, along with a mix of negative events that include the 1997 financial crisis, 9/11 and its fallout, a depressed economy, shrinking markets, the Gulf War, SARS, and the risk of the Asian bird flu pandemic, there continues to be significant pressure on cost reduction driven by ever-increasing competition. It's therefore no surprise that DBS increasingly sees service as a key differentiator in attracting and retaining profitable customers.

Immediately following the 1997 Asian financial crisis, DBS initiated an extensive operational review and recognized that the marketplace delivery of its financial products is based upon a hybrid of centralized, decentralized, and regional back offices that enable the front-office customer servicing and support functions. On the basis of benchmarking, DBS was able to define the following key performance characteristics for its retail bank service delivery:

Centralized processing. Allowing "customer-facing" units to focus on serving the customer, supported by centralized back-office units to perform backroom functions.

High quality of processes. Achieved through the implementation of proven quality models, such as Six Sigma and ISO 9000, to fix root causes of poor quality and supported by the implementation of metrics-based performance tracking.

High straight-through processing. Minimizing manual intervention by designing technology-enabled straight-through processes.

Regional processing. Consolidating processing regionwide to achieve scale-driven cost reduction.

Third-party involvement. Building partnerships with vendors to create an extended enterprise that enables the efficient and effective outsourcing of noncore functions.

Empowered workforce. Implementing objective and reliable measurement systems to enable pay-for-performance.

In 1999, in response to these challenges, DBS created a processing-and-servicing (P&S) strategy and organization whose objectives were to:

- Consolidate P&S capabilities and platforms where appropriate, to achieve greater efficiency and economies of scale
- Recognize that *service* is the *key differentiator* and transform "backroom operations" into "centers of excellence"
- Allow frontline employees to concentrate on marketing and sales-related activities rather than administration and processing
- Create an operational infrastructure blueprint that supports the DBS regional mission

The P&S journey over the last six years has enabled the bank to achieve significant benefits with respect to its objective to operate at a world-class level, and it is now one of the leading banks in the region.

Our final real-life success story, for now, features Marks & Spencer Money,[9] a midsized financial services organization that provides credit cards, insurance, and loans and savings products in the United Kingdom. The organization was formerly part of the Marks & Spencer retail chain, prior to its sale to HSBC at the end of 2004.

Its story as another fast follower is particularly interesting and demonstrates that organizations don't need to be into a multiyear Six Sigma or Lean implementation before the benefits of taking a strong core process-focused approach can yield results.

The members of the leadership team recognized that if their initial "proof-of-concept" project was to be a successful launch pad for the use of Six Sigma more broadly across the organization, the project had to satisfy five key criteria. In short, it had to:

- Deliver a significant business impact
- Align with, and be supportive of, the company's key operational strategies—one of which was to launch a credit card
- Focus on an end-to-end process that was easily defined and understood
- Have cross-functional impact
- Have very strong senior leadership sponsorship and support

With these criteria in mind and after initial analysis and the presentation of recommendations, the team was given the mandate to proceed with a Six Sigma effort focusing on the end-to-end new customer acquisition process.

The project was immensely successful, generating total cost reduction and additional revenue-generation benefits in excess of £1 million and ensuring the successful launch of the company's new credit card offering.

On the basis of this success, the six full-time employees that compose this relatively small team have now broadened their end-to-end process analysis and infrastructure efforts. They have defined and successfully proposed eight core processes to the senior leadership team and developed performance dashboards for at least half of these, which have enabled them to identify further high-impact and high-priority projects that are now under way.

Closing Comments

This chapter clearly illustrates the value that financial services organizations of different sizes, operating in different subindustries and geographies, can realize from using Six Sigma. Arguably, Bank of America is now the service-transactional leader in the deployment of Six Sigma within the financial services industry. And others are looking to emulate Bank of America's success, as they strive to beat their competitors.

This leaves us with several key questions to be answered in the following sections of our book:

1. What is *world class*, and what is needed to get there?
2. How are financial services organizations using Six Sigma, Lean and other methodologies to transform and improve their businesses?
3. What does the future hold for financial services organizations, and how does business process excellence enable them to succeed?

Notes

1. Michael Hammer, "Business Processes in Financial Services," Microsoft white paper (September 2003).
2. The sources for this section are Bank of America Annual Reports to Shareholders, *Charlotte Observer* (July 2005), Bank of America 2Q05 earnings release, Bank of America investor presentation (August 2005), *Fortune* (September 2005), Bank of America Web site, www.sixsigmacompanies.com, and www.hoovers.com.
3. We'll describe Bank of America's use of Hoshin-Kanri in detail in Chapter 6. For now, it's sufficient to know that it's a very effective method for seamlessly planning and evaluating activities performed in an organization with respect to the overarching strategies of the organization.
4. Additional information on the Bank of America deployment can be found in the recent book by Ronald Snee and Roger Hoerl, *Six Sigma Beyond the Factory Floor*, Upper Saddle River, NJ: Pearson Prentice Hall, 2006.
5. The sources for this section include JPMorgan Chase Annual Reports to Shareholders; Bill Stoneman, John R. Engen, and Kenneth Cline, "Perilous Passage?" *BAI Banking Strategies*, vol. LXXVII, no. VI (November/December 2001); JPMorgan Chase Web site; and www.sixsigmacompanies.com.
6. In this section, the sources are American Express Annual Reports to Shareholders; talking points prepared for presentation to the Lehman Brothers Financial Services Conference by American Express executive vice president and chief financial officer Gary Crittenden; www.sixsigmacompanies.com; www.bloomberg.com

7. In this section, the sources are Countrywide Financial Corporation Annual Reports to Shareholders; www.sixsigmacompanies.com; and www.hoovers.com.
8. The source of this section is DBS, "The Transformation Bank," presentation made at the 2004 Asian Six Sigma Summit (presenter unknown).
9. The material in this section is taken from Sue Brown, "Initial Implementation of Six Sigma at Marks & Spencer Money," IQPC Six Sigma Summit, London (2004).

4

What Does *World Class* <u>Really</u> Mean?

T O EVEN ATTEMPT to answer this question probably requires a book in itself, and so the purpose of this chapter is to simply introduce the term *world class* and offer some suggestions on how the question might be answered. In doing so, we'll consider the question's importance for achieving business process excellence within the context of today's financial services industry.

We'll continue to refer to the theme of world-class business process excellence throughout the rest of this book. In addition, in the final section of the book titled "The Future of Business Process Excellence in Financial Services," you'll find a detailed view of the organizational and operational characteristics that we would expect to see in financial services organizations that claim to have achieved world-class business process excellence—so, if you can't wait, turn to the final section now!

In our experience, the term *world class* is often overused, and it's also highly ambiguous. In fact, if you were to conduct a Google search on various world-class–related search strings—as we have done[1]—you might get results similar to the ones shown in Box 4.1.

So what does "world-class performance in financial services" *really* mean? The Hackett Group[2] is a global business advisory firm that provides insight and advice obtained from over 3,500 benchmark studies conducted over the last 14 years. Its financial services clients include

Box 4.1

Search String	Hits
"what is world class"	795,000,000
"what is world-class performance"	198,000,000
"what is world-class performance in financial services"	74,400,000
"world-class performance"	380,000
"world-class financial services"	17,600
"world-class banking"	9,680
"world-class performance in financial services"	0

ABN AMRO, Bank of America, Charles Schwab, Citigroup, Merrill Lynch, Royal Bank of Scotland, and UBS.

The Hackett Group defines *world class* as, "Companies ranking in the top 25 percent in efficiency and effectiveness metrics. These companies have been able to strike a balance of efficiency and effectiveness that is appropriate for their business goals and operating model." World-class efficiency is characterized by the deliberate creation of and adherence to a strategy for operating in the lowest-cost manner possible. World-class effectiveness is characterized by a strategy for delivering the highest possible levels of value and service to the business.

The Hackett Group uses the model shown in Figure 4.1 to understand and evaluate the levels of performance its client organizations achieve.

We believe that there are three key questions that financial services organizations must continually ask on the subject of world-class performance:

1. *Who* truly defines *world class?* We would suggest that it's customers and shareholders who should define this performance level.
2. *What* does *world-class performance* really mean? We would suggest that performing within the top 25 percent is *"high in class,"* but is it really *world class?* Should organizations be performing in the top 10 percent to legitimately claim to be world class?
3. If we're not performing at world-class levels today, *how* and *when* do we get there, and will it still be considered world class when we do?

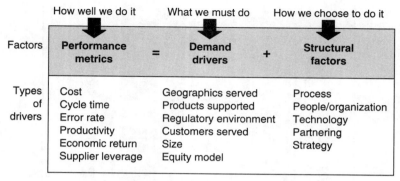

Figure 4.1   Performance evaluation model
Hackett benchmarks focus on measuring the drivers of world-class
performance.

In our research to better understand what *world class* really means, we
utilized a widely recognized resource, the American Customer Satisfaction Index. The ACSI was established in 1994 "to provide a uniform and
independent measure of household consumption experience"
(www.theacsi.com). ACSI tracks trends in customer satisfaction
and provides valuable measurements that are used by companies
and government agencies. The ACSI is produced by the Stephen
M. Ross Business School at the University of Michigan, in partnership
with the American Society for Quality (ASQ) and CFI Group, an international consulting firm.

Table 4.1 shows the results for the finance and insurance, banks, and
brokerage segments of the U.S. financial services market over the last 12
years; consumers' perceptions are shown on a scale of 0 to 100 percent
favorable.

According to www.theacsi.org, the "ACSI model is a set of causal
equations that link customer expectations, perceived quality, and perceived value to customer satisfaction. In turn, satisfaction is linked to
consequences as defined by customer complaints and customer loyalty—measured by price tolerance and customer retention." Since for
most companies, repeat customers are major contributors to profit, the
linkage between satisfaction, perceived quality, and perceived value is
critically important. "Thus, customer retention is a key to financial performance. By combining it with certain financial data, ACSI corporate

Table 4.1

	Baseline*	Q4 1994	Q4 1995	Q4 1996	Q4 1997	Q4 1998	Q4 1999	Q4 2000	Q4 2001	Q4 2002	Q4 2003	Q4 2004	Q4 2005	Previous Year % Changes	First Year % Changes
FINANCE & INSURANCE	78.5	74.8	74.1	74.5	74.6	74.4	73.9	74.4	73.3	73.8	74.7	73.4	73.9	0.7%	-5.9%
Banks	74	74	74	72	71	70	68	70	72	74	75	75	75	0.0%	1.4%
Wachovia Corporation	76	75	73	71	74	68	68	66	72	73	76	78	79	1.3%	3.9%
All Others	75	76	77	77	74	73	70	72	74	76	76	77	78	1.3%	4.0%
Bank of America Corporation	72	68	67	65	61	62	61	63	68	70	74	72	72	0.0%	0.0%
JPMorgan Chase & Co. (formerly Bank One)	77	75	74	69	70	68	66	70	66	70	70	70	70	0.0%	-9.1%
Wells Fargo & Company	71	69	71	65	62	67	65	67	66	69	68	70	67	-4.3%	-5.6%

	Baseline*	Q4 1994	Q4 1995	Q4 1996	Q4 1997	Q4 1998	Q4 1999	Q4 2000	Q4 2001	Q4 2002	Q4 2003	Q4 2004	Q4 2005	Previous Year % Changes	First Year % Changes
Brokerage	NM	NM	NM	NM	NM	NM	NM	72	69	73	76	75	76	1.3%	5.6%
All Others	NM	NM	NM	NM	NM	NM	NM	70	65	73	77	78	79	1.3%	12.9%
The Charles Schwab Corporation	NM	NM	NM	NM	NM	NM	NM	76	72	76	75	71	74	4.2%	-2.6%
E*TRADE Financial Corp.	NM	NM	NM	NM	NM	NM	NM	66	66	69	71	70	71	1.4%	7.6%

Note. The ACSI is updated quarterly, with results for a different set of industries each quarter. The *All Others* score for an industry represents the remainder of the total industry market share, less the market shares of the ACSI-measured companies. It is an aggregate of a representative number of customer interviews from each of potentially hundreds of smaller companies within the industry.

subscribers are able to calculate the net present value of their company's customer base as an asset over time."[3]

The significant differences in ACSI scores among the measured financial service organizations suggest that quality methods such as Six Sigma and Lean do indeed contribute to superior customer experiences. According to Professor Claus Fornell, the creator of ACSI:

Retail banking remains at an all-time high of 75 for a third straight year, with Wachovia [remember its story?] continuing to lead, up 1 percent to 79. Contrary to what is often the case, recent mergers do not appear to have had much effect on customer satisfaction. JPMorgan Chase, which acquired Bank One in 2004 to become the third largest bank in the U.S., posts a score of 70 for a fourth straight year. Customer satisfaction with Bank of America, the nation's second largest bank, dropped in 2004 after acquiring Fleet Boston, but holds steady for 2005. Wells Fargo has made roughly 50 acquisitions since 1998, mostly of small local banks and has also been at or near the bottom of the industry in customer satisfaction. This year Wells Fargo drops further; its ACSI falls 4 percent to 67, the lowest score for any bank since 2001. Frequent merger activity over many years is consistent with lower customer satisfaction, as the process of integrating and reorganizing new banks is a major challenge.

The overall U.S. score for the fourth quarter of 2005 was 73.5, which shows that while many financial services companies were above the average, they were by no means displaying a significant or world-class service offering in the eyes of their customers, especially when compared with high-scoring e-commerce retail service darlings such as Amazon.com or BarnesandNobles.com, which each scored 87.

So how else can we define *world class*?

The scoring model for the U.S.–based Malcolm Baldrige National Quality Award[4] (a model for assessing an organization's quality and performance that has been followed by many other countries around the world), may offer us a benchmark for comparison. While this is only one component of a very thorough examination and review process used by the MBNQA examiners, the concepts apply for this discussion on world class as well. To achieve the top scores in this category, an organization needs to demonstrate 90, 95, or 100 percent in the following:

- An effective, systematic approach, fully responsive to the multiple requirements of the item, is evident.
- The approach is fully deployed without significant weaknesses or gaps in any areas or work units.
- Fact-based, systematic evaluation and improvement and organizational learning are key organization-wide tools; refinement and innovation, backed by analysis and sharing, are evident throughout the organization.
- The approach is well integrated with your organizational needs identified in response to the other criteria items.

Any organization that achieves a score above 90 percent in any of the seven categories of the MBNQA performance excellence assessment criteria would definitely have to be considered world class. At this time none of the major U.S. financial services corporations have received this prestigious award as a result of their process improvement efforts. In 2003 the MBNQA service category was won by Caterpillar Financial Services Corporation, in 1997 by Merrill Lynch Credit Corp., and in 1992 by AT&T Universal Card Services, which has since been absorbed by Citigroup.

So what does *world class* really mean?

In his landmark book, *Built to Last,* Jim Collins presents the 12 shattered myths of visionary companies. His exposition on myth number 10 is most fitting here:

Myth 10: The most successful companies focus on primarily beating the competition.

Reality: Visionary companies focus primarily on beating themselves. Success and beating competitors comes to the visionary companies not so much as the end goal, but as the result of relentlessly asking the question, "How can we improve ourselves to do better tomorrow than we did today?" And they have asked this question day in and day out—as a disciplined way of life—in some cases for over a 150 years . . .[5]

The concept of world class is nothing more than a constantly moving and improving benchmark against which organizations can compare their performance. Yet it's a vital data point for financial services organizations striving to define and achieve business process excellence for their organizations.

Closing Comments on Part I

The global financial services industry is, and will continue to be, engendered by significant change and complexity. It is clear there is substantial room for improvement in the eyes of the customer for the industry as a whole. We believe the driving forces and success stories we've described present a compelling argument for organizations to establish a business process excellence agenda that is based on a fully integrated package of leading methods, tools, and techniques to achieve superior performance.

In addressing the topics in this opening part of our book, we hope to have provided a comprehensive picture of the challenges and opportunities that exist within the financial services industry today.

We'll now explore how business process excellence approaches such as Six Sigma, Lean, and other methods for achieving and assessing business improvements can be successfully used to achieve higher levels of process performance and better business results.

Notes

1. www.google.com. Search conducted on March 26, 2006, on Google's U.K. engine.
2. www.thehackettgroup.com.
3. www.theacsi.com
4. www.quality.nist.gov
5. James C. Collins, Jerry I. Porras, *Built to Last: Successful Habits of Visionary Companies* (New York: Harper Business, 1997).

2

Process Leadership

Make your theory as simple as possible,
but no simpler.
—A. Einstein

Introduction

In the second part of our book, we will explore how financial services organizations are driving results using Six Sigma, Lean, and other proven business improvement techniques to achieve business process excellence.

All Models Are Wrong, but Some Are Useful[1]

We would like to start by introducing a model that will serve as a structure to explain our ideas. In developing this model, we have deliberately made it *methodology-neutral*; in other words, it's not specific to Six Sigma, Business Process Management, Lean, or any other improvement methodology, although we've embedded the underlying themes of each of those methods in it.

In fact, there are various ways in which we could have framed the key components of our business process excellence model, and we considered several approaches before settling on the use of these three key themes: *process leadership, process knowledge,* and *process execution.*

The entire model is, as one would expect, driven by the requirements of key marketplace constituents—*customers, shareholders,* and *regulators.* The entire focus of the model is to achieve business *process results* that continually shape and inform the expectations and future requirements of the key marketplace constituents in a closed-loop relationship (see Figure P2.1).

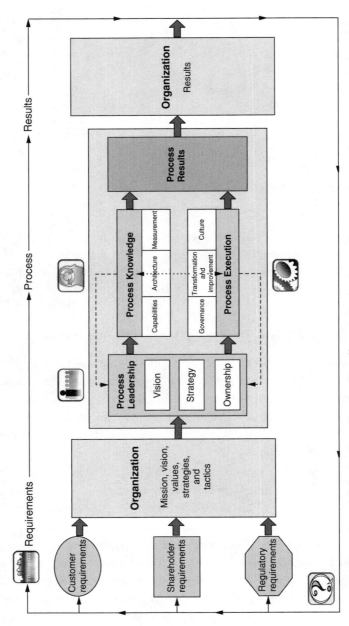

Figure P2.1 A model for Business Process Excellence

Drilling down farther, we will break the key themes into key requirements:

> Within process leadership, we will explore three key requirements to achieve business process excellence: *process vision, process strategy,* and *process ownership.*
>
> Within process knowledge, we will explore the three key requirements of *process capability, process architecture,* and *process measurement.*
>
> Within process execution, we will explore the three key requirements of *process governance, process transformation and improvement,* and *process culture.*

We have set aside an entire part of our book for each *key theme,* and within each part we have set aside a chapter for each *key requirement.* Our intent is to explain the importance of each requirement for achieving business process excellence and provide examples of how leading exponents within financial services organizations are utilizing Six Sigma, Lean, and BPM approaches to address these requirements. In taking this approach, we hope to provide a simple framework, an explanation, and real-life examples to help guide your Six Sigma, Lean, and BPM-based business process excellence efforts.

In summary, the key themes and requirements for successfully achieving business process excellence are outlined below:

Process Leadership

- *Process vision.* "We have a vision for each end-to-end process, fully aligned with the business strategy."
- *Process strategy.* "We have a structured plan to achieve our process vision(s)."
- *Process ownership.* "We have a senior leader accountable for each end-to-end process."

Process Knowledge

- *Process capabilities.* "We have the resources, skills, and capabilities to achieve our business process excellence objectives."

- *Process architecture.* "We understand our organization's end-to-end processes and how they fit together to maximize value."
- *Process measurement.* "We have *a balanced set of* measurements for each of our end-to-end processes."

Process Execution

- *Process governance.* "We have end-to-end process governance and accountabilities."
- *Process transformation and improvement.* "We use leading methods, tools, and techniques to systematically transform and improve our end-to-end processes."
- *Process culture.* "We have an organizational culture that enables our business process excellence efforts to flourish and succeed."

Let's start by exploring *process leadership.*

We believe that leaders driving business process excellence efforts in today's highly complex and competitive financial services environment require exceptional skills to fully realize the value that their customers and shareholders demand and expect.

Although a lot of great work is being done by many highly committed people in many organizations around the world today, we haven't, at this point, identified a financial services organization that can legitimately claim to have achieved true business process excellence as we're defining it. If you know of such an organization, please let us know!

However, as we have said, there are many financial services organizations using techniques such as Six Sigma and Lean in the pursuit of business process excellence. So what is it that differentiates the successful organizations—such as those whose success stories we described in the earlier part of this book—from others?

While the various methods, tools, and techniques available to achieve business process excellence may be somewhat different from one another, there is one common, unifying theme that's a critical success factor for all of them, and that's *leadership.*

Achieving business process excellence in financial services organizations, or any other type of organization for that matter, is not just about using the most powerful process management, improvement, and transformation methods, such as Lean and Six Sigma. Although these approaches have a key role to play, *they are a means to an end and not an end in themselves.* In some financial services organizations, this simple fact tends to get overlooked, and process improvement people get caught up in the "beauty" of the method, or the "application" of the tool, rather than the *endgame* of what it is they're trying to achieve—namely, improved processes that will create significantly enhanced value for their customers and key stakeholders. Perhaps you've witnessed this in your own organization.

The financial services organizations that are the leading Lean and Six Sigma proponents today go way beyond methods, tools, and techniques. At the heart of their approaches is an acknowledgment that the fundamentals of how their business processes are defined, designed, measured, managed, and continually improved and transformed must be radically changed. These are the organizations that are on the leading edge of business process excellence.

Consider, for example, comments made by U.S. Bancorp vice chairman Richard K. Davis.[2] Davis is in charge of consumer banking and payment services at the Minneapolis-based, multistate financial holding company, which provides a full range of financial services with assets of $195 billion in 2004 and sales of almost $15 billion. Davis notes:

> *Believing [in customer service] is not all of it, but if you don't believe, you can't get started.... It's not a promotion or campaign.... It can't be the item of the year. It has to be part of everything you do.... A robust customer service program involves technology and systems; HR policies; incentive programs; marketing and customer communication; and tracking and monitoring systems. What gets counted, gets done.*

While purists might argue that the language is not Six Sigma or Lean, the messages are clear. Leaders such as Richard K. Davis recognize and understand the value of cross-functional collaboration to achieve robust customer service. Increasingly, financial services organizations are cutting through functional layers, decision making, operational systems, and old ways of doing things to expose the essential processes and the key attributes of those processes that their customers truly value.

And once they fully understand—often for the first time—how the key things that they make and do actually create and deliver value for their customers (and other key stakeholders), they set in place business process excellence techniques such as Lean and Six Sigma to help them continually meet or exceed customers' requirements. This leadership mindset requires outstanding vision, commitment, and tenacity.

Notes

1. George E. P. Box.
2. "BAI's SmartTactics for Profitable Retail Delivery Conference," Las Vegas, NV.

5

Defining a Vision

IN THIS CHAPTER, we'll discuss the importance of process vision and describe how organizations can establish a vision for each of their core end-to-end processes, fully aligned with their business strategy. We can think about shaping such an integrated vision in two ways.

First, many financial services organizations that have embarked upon a significant process improvement and transformation effort of any description have found it very helpful to create a *vision* of where they're trying to get to. It's a good way to describe what the organization is striving for and can be a powerful way to mobilize and energize the organization for the journey ahead.

Second, it's critical that any business improvement or transformation effort using methods such as Lean or Six Sigma be integrally linked to the organization's overall *business strategy*—the big things that the organization is going to do—and that it is appropriately aligned with any existing business process improvement or change initiatives.

Given the importance of an integrated vision, it's particularly interesting to note that most of the financial services organizations we surveyed have not yet established a vision or long-term strategic goals for each of their core end-to-end processes. In fact, less than 10 percent indicated that they had taken such an approach to all of their core end-to-end processes at this time, although 36 percent of organizations had initiated this work for some of their processes. A further 18 percent indicated they were just piloting or beginning now.

An excellent approach that a number of financial services organizations are increasingly taking is to create a "future-state picture" for each of their core end-to-end processes. We'll refer to this as a *process point of arrival (POA),* as this language seems to be widely used by a number of organizations today.

These process POAs should ideally explain what each process would look like—the process vision—in order to address the requirements of the organization's business improvement and transformation objectives. It's really best if they can be crafted as a set of five to seven key metrics (see Figure 5.1). In many financial services organizations these are referred to as *key performance indicators (KPIs).*

As organizations start to create their process POAs, they often realize that they don't have all the data and information they require. Some organizations choose to use *proxy* measures—metrics that go some way to doing the job of the KPIs they really need. Or they may choose, as a placeholder, to simply describe the *process POAs* by using words until they've obtained the KPI data they need.

Given the newness of such an approach for many financial services organizations, it's highly likely that one of the first things that will need to be done is to commission resources to obtain the data that are required in order to set targets and track performance over time. This

	Process performance	
	Today	POA
Applications processed	10 million	25 million
Rolled throughput yield	60%	90%
Sigma level	3.2	6.0
Process-cycle efficiency	5%	50%
Unit cost	10.0 c	6.0 c
Customer satisfaction	80%	>95%

Figure 5.1 Customer acquisition end-to-end process
An example of key performance indicators (KPI) for a
sample process.

may seem arduous and unnecessary, but by framing process POAs in this way, organizations will be able to track their progress over time and easily communicate successes and areas of focus going forward. Simply put, it is the only way that organizations can verify they are working on the most important improvement opportunities.

As part of the research effort for this book we conducted an interview with Laura Currier, senior vice president of Customer Quality at FESCo., a division of Fidelity Investments, to discuss its deployment and the lessons it learned from its journey. Laura remarked that, "After two years of doing projects, with considerable success and momentum, we are now realizing that projects will not be enough to get us where we want to be. . . . We need to build a robust quality management system. Once we do that, our rate of improvement should increase dramatically."

Closing Comments on Process Vision

The importance of an integrated vision that links a business process excellence approach (such as Six Sigma) with an organization's overall business strategy is a critical first step. The consequences of not establishing such a linkage often result in employees' asking some very reasonable questions, such as, "How does this fit with XYZ?" or "How serious are we about this?" or making comments such as, "I don't have time for this—*I'm too busy executing our strategy!*"

Interestingly, this is the chapter of our book that we're least happy with, quite simply because we've been unable to find any substantial real-world examples of what we're describing and advocating, even though some of the survey respondents (see the opening of this section) had noted that they had established process visions or were beginning to pursue this effort. While there are plenty of examples of organizations using such approaches as vision and mission statements (who doesn't have one of these framed on a wall somewhere?), the translation of these approaches into specific operational vision statements for each core value-creating process doesn't appear to exist in the way we have defined it here. In his landmark *Harvard Business Review* article, "Leading Change: Why Transformation Efforts Fail," John Kotter, retired Kono- suke Professor of Leadership at the Harvard Business School, identifies the absence of a vision as a key error that organizations commit, causing transformation efforts to fail. Kotter goes further to state, "If you can't communicate the vision to someone in five minutes or less and get a reaction that signifies both understanding and interest, you are not yet done with this phase of the transformation process."[1] This is a critical gap in an organization's ability to take its improvement programs to the next level. The organizations that truly do aspire to be world class will be those that set a vision for each process and that values that process as a strategic asset. We'll explore the topic of processes as strategic assets in the next chapter.

For now, we'll simply express our view that an organization's employees—and others involved in end-to-end processes such as third-party suppliers, vendors, and business partners—need to understand what the vision is for the process(es) in which they work and that the organization is serious about the effort. The key messages need to be communicated and reinforced by the most senior leaders in the organization, continually and thoughtfully, throughout the process excellence journey.

Notes

1. John P. Kotter, "Leading Change: Why Transformation Efforts Fail," *Harvard Business Review*, March–April 1995.

CHAPTER

Shaping a Strategy

P RIOR TO FORMULATING a process strategy, an organization should establish its business process excellence vision and fully align the process POAs with the overall business strategy. Now it is ready to translate that vision into an operational strategy—a process strategy to ensure successful execution. In this chapter, we'll explain the importance of *process strategy* and describe how some leading financial services organizations are going about establishing a structured plan to achieve their process vision.

Processes as Strategic Assets

Our "big" hypothesis is that, in general, business processes are severely suboptimized in most financial services organizations today. This is further compounded by our view that end-to-end core processes are rarely perceived as—or managed as—strategic assets. That's a rather sweeping statement; perhaps we should clarify what we mean here. Our observation is that in most financial services organizations, a weak link, at best, exists between the overall *business strategy* and the *operational strategies, processes,* and *activities* that are followed day in, day out—supposedly in support of successfully achieving the business strategy.

Today, it's almost certain that if a seamless translation of business strategy to operational execution is being made at all, it is being made within the context of the functional organization—for example, "Here's what an organization's business strategy means Sales now needs to do," or, "Here's what an organization's business strategy means Operations now needs to do." In our experience, there is very little evidence to indicate that business strategy is translated into, "So this is what we now need to do across our *end-to-end core processes to successfully achieve our strategic objectives.*" In fact, in our view, most financial services organizations, even if they have defined their end-to-end core processes, are not measuring, managing, improving, or redesigning their service delivery across the end-to-end supply chain.

In most financial services organizations today, strategy execution is taking place within each separate organizational function (e.g., Sales, Operations) as opposed to across the *end-to-end processes* that customers actually experience throughout the tenure of their relationship with an organization. We suspect that this may well be the case with *your* organization.

Consequently, many financial services organizations are failing to maximize the value-creation opportunities that exist across their end-to-end core processes—you might recall some of the observations made by the IBM Institute of Value Management on Straight-Through Processing noted in Chapter 2. Typically in financial services organizations, the very nature of the *environment* and the *work flow* means that *process consciousness* is more challenging to establish and maintain than in a manufacturing environment.

To summarize, our view is that most financial services organizations today are not managing their delivery processes as *strategic value–creating assets* to achieve increased customer satisfaction and loyalty—but rather as a set of disparate, isolated functional delivery mechanisms that, over time, naturally deteriorate in their ability to satisfy customers and create loyalty-based value.

Strategy Is Execution

Our survey findings support a number of the assertions we have just made.

Although 80 percent of organizations have established shareholder-focused goals for the next three years or longer at an organizational level, only 25 percent have established shareholder-focused goals for *every* core end-to-end process. A further 50 percent indicated that shareholder-focused goals had been established for *some* of their documented core end-to-end processes.

With regard to customer-focused goals, the picture is similar. While 70 percent of organizations have established customer-focused goals for the next three years or longer at an organizational level, only 10 percent have established customer-focused goals for *every* core end-to-end process—the things that customers actually experience! A further 45 percent indicated that customer-focused goals had been established for *some* of their documented core end-to-end processes.

We also noted that only 36 percent of organizations have established a comprehensive multigenerational plan to guide the execution of their process transformation and improvement efforts. So what approaches can be taken to better connect an organization's business process excellence vision with the strategies and actions that it takes in order to achieve that vision?

Of all the financial services organizations we've researched and surveyed in the development of this book, we believe that Bank of America has the best approach for linking vision, strategy, and execution. Joe Valasquez, former Bank of America **Bank of America** senior vice president of quality and productivity, explains their approach:

Six Sigma is best deployed into an organization's strategy when it is the "how to deploy" of the strategy. Starting with the organizational strategy sets the tone for the entire organization. We use the Hoshin planning process for our strategic plan development and the Kanri process as our periodic management methodology. Put together, this is the Hoshin Kanri process which roughly translated means "compass" and "directed."

Hoshin plans help key leaders focus on the vision for the company, ways to drive the breakthrough strategies to achieve the vision and crisply defined tactics for each strategy. Metrics are assigned to define success and measure progress. Planning at every subordinate level is required to demonstrate how it is aligned to the plan above it, creating a cascade in which every strategy, tactic and metric can ultimately be connected to the company's master plan.

An effective organizational strategy is surprisingly simple in structure. The beauty of a great plan is its simplicity. Transforming a complex annual plan into a concise document requires focusing on the critical few.

In order to achieve the plan, the Six Sigma skill set and methodology are required to achieve the breakthrough goals. Some plans identify training and yield targets (yield is a measure of number trained versus number certified) for Six Sigma. The real linkage of strategic plan to Six Sigma is that it is difficult to achieve breakthrough goals in defects, speed and customer delight without using Six Sigma tools.[1]

Figure 6.1 shows the Hoshin-Kanri schematic[2] that Bank of America uses to facilitate the planning and review process described. Note the three key components—1.0 Set Direction, 2.0 Align the Organization, and 3.0 Manage Performance—and the closed-loop relationship between Kanri and Hoshin.

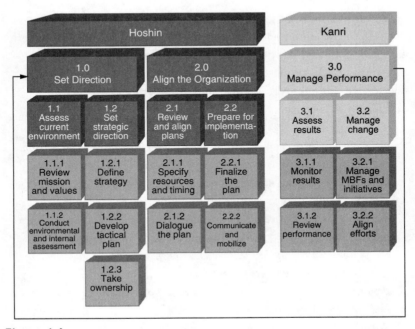

Figure 6.1
Bank of America *Hoshin-Kanri* planning process

Linking an organization's business process excellence journey to its business *vision* and *strategy* sends the right message from the start—we're serious about this! Regular and frequent communications and other visible actions from senior leaders will be critical in reinforcing the organization's commitment to the effort.

If Strategy Is Execution, How Can Progress Be Assessed?

"We've been improving this process for a long time. But . . . just how do we know whether we're making progress? Where do we stand?"

As process management efforts and initiatives grow over time, a concern that management and practitioners share is how to evaluate the outcome of collective improvements and, in effect, the overall status of any given end-to-end process. There are many different approaches a financial services organization can take to assess progress on its business process excellence journey.

One response to this concern is the burgeoning field of *process management maturity*. Processes can and do evolve to achieve higher levels of performance. The changes required to bring about the better performance are the subject matter of process improvement methods, reengineering, new technologies, and the myriad tools and techniques available to process management practitioners. So, then, processes go through stages of development in our quest to take them "to the next level."

At American Express (AXP), Roberto Saco, vice president of strategic planning, is, in our view, engaged in work at the very leading edge of assessing process management maturity within the financial services industry. Roberto is well placed to lead such work; he served as a Baldrige examiner from 1994 to 2001, during which time he assessed more than 80 firms in different industry sectors, including several major banks. More recently, as the leader for AXP's Six Sigma deployment  across the Latin America region, he has been successfully leading his team on an initiative to define, measure, and track the organization's process management maturity.

Over the next few pages, Roberto describes the approach he and his colleagues have taken, the challenges they've identified and overcome, and the results they have been able to achieve. We think you'll find his contribution, for which we are very grateful, highly interesting.

The maturity model that Roberto and his team designed and piloted at American Express and that they named *PM³ (process management maturity model)* is an example of a home-grown, prescriptive model applied to individual processes, and it will serve as an illustration of maturity models and their application. This model has now been put into practice by Roberto and his Master Black Belts, and PM³ answers those lingering concerns that many Six Sigma leaders regularly ask: *"Are we on the right track?" "Are we moving fast enough?" "What do we do next?"*

Introduction to PM³

Consider the following situation.

A cross-functional task force had been working in making improvements to the AXP Mexico payments process for more than two years. These are the payments made by AXP card members to settle their monthly credit card bills. In Mexico, logistics for the payment process are rather complicated by several long-standing issues having to do with poor postal system infrastructure, macroeconomic parameters that require card members to pay their bills within a very short time frame, banking regulations, and an outdated payments clearinghouse, as well as the complexity of the product itself, which allows card members to pay in a variety of formats and currencies.

Mexico is, by some counts, AXP's largest market outside the United States, and the payment process churns several billion dollars through its "pipelines." It is not a minor or trivial process, and on any importance or performance grid, it ranks very high. Six Sigma and other process improvement tools had been applied. Several dozen improvement projects were implemented over the course of the two years. And more importantly, a very sound business strategy was crafted to provide customers with better access to the AXP payment network. Costs, customer satisfaction, and process compliance had all been significantly improved in this time. Some task force members, however, believed that they had reached an impasse, and progress had slowed down.

The assessment model and exercise we designed, then, had the simple purpose of generating additional impetus for change. It was more of a discovery intervention in that the process teams and task force were to self-assess their end-to-end process, to discover areas of strengths and opportunities for improvement, and from these to create a list of priorities for further action. The structure of the model would be very familiar to anyone acquainted with the United States Malcolm Baldrige National Quality Award performance excellence assessment,[3] and that's not by accident, drawing on many years of experience as a national quality award senior examiner to design the basic structure of PM^3.

PM^3: The Model

Conceptually, the model can be depicted graphically, as shown in Figure 6.2. As you can see from the figure, the model has five clusters: The *ownership and governance* cluster establishes direction for process management. The *efficiency drivers* cluster, together with the *stakeholder drivers* cluster—as identified and determined by the process owners—impacts and influences *comprehensive process results*. And the entire model is supported and enabled by the *process understanding* cluster via capability, control, improvement, and assessment.

The notion of *process understanding* is key in that it's the field in which the other clusters operate. Without process understanding, there is no system, only independent clusters suboptimizing each other's effectiveness in the organization. Each cluster, in turn, comprises several process features. For example, the ownership and governance clus-

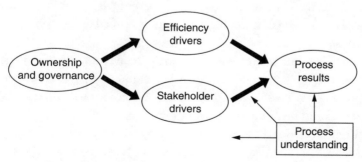

Figure 6.2 Building blocks or clusters and their relationships

ter is composed of *process ownership, process performance requirements,* and *baseline and benchmark.* Here are these three features expressed as a desirable end state.

- *Process ownership.* An end-to-end process owner with accountability for the entire supply chain has been assigned and is acting the role. There is process governance, documented and deployed, that dictates how the process must be run. A process vision, outlining an ideal state for the process, is understood, communicated, and documented.
- *Process performance requirements.* A balanced measurement system is in place that provides constant measurements of the metrics that drive and are derived from the processes. We also have targets (requirements) for each metric. The targets have been validated to comply with customer and shareholder specifications, where applicable.
- *Baseline and benchmark.* We have a point-of-departure measurement for all metrics, including process capability, with which we will compare to assess the impact and progress of our initiatives. We know the point of arrival for each metric, and we have identified opportunities to help us get there. We have also compared our process performance with other regions and competitors performance.

In all, fifteen features are assessed in these five clusters. The assessment requires that each feature be scored according to the Baldrige-based scoring guidelines presented in Figure 6.3. The features in all the clusters, except process results, are evaluated using the approach and deployment dimensions of the guidelines. In other words, does the process show evidence of the requirements set forth in the description of each feature, and is the deployment widely spread to the appropriate subprocesses?

As a result, every one of the 15 features receives a score (0–100 percent), and the overall process receives a weighted score (maximum of 1,000 points) and designation. For example, one of our processes, say process X, could be rated as shown in Figure 6.4.

As Figure 6.4 clearly shows, process X is—barely—in the developmental level and needs a lot of work. Many features are in the early stages of development, and the overall score for the process is 265. The

	Approach	Deployment	Results
Primeval (0%)	No systematic approach	Anecdotal, undocumented	No results or poor results
Initial (10–20%)	Limited systematic approach, transition from reactive to improvement oriented	Major gaps in development exist. Few units use improvement tactics, but many are not.	Results not reported for many to most areas of importance. Positive results for a few areas.
In Development (30–40%)	An effective systematic approach is clearly in place. Emphasis on prevention. Beginning of systematic evaluation and improvement is evident. Random improvements have been made.	A few major gaps in deployment exist. Minor requirements not addressed. Many work units in early stages of development.	Results are reported for most key areas of importance. Early stage of developing trends and obtaining comparative information.
Competitive (50–60%)	Systematic approach is fully developed and in place. Prevention and fact-based improvement system includes process evaluation. No systematic refinements are in place.	No major gaps in development exist. Few work units still be in the early stages of development.	Results are reported for most areas of importance to the organization's key requirements. Good performance levels show areas of strength relative to benchmarks.
Superior (70–80%)	An effective, preventive, fact-based, integrated improvement system is fully developed and clearly responsive to current and changing business needs. Systematic evaluation and improvement cycles are evident. A few innovative refinements are evident.	No major gaps in development with many work units in the advanced stages of development. Overall requirements are addressed and practiced by all components.	Results are reported for most areas of importance to the organization's key requirements. Excellent performance is reported and sustained in many of those areas relative to benchmarks. Some areas of leadership are demonstrated.
World-class (70–80%)	A preventive, fact-based, integrated quality system is fully developed and systematically refined through evaluation and improvement cycles to meet current and changing business needs. Many innovative processes with many refinements are evident.	Approach is fully deployed with most to all work units in the advanced stages of development. All requirements are addressed and practiced by all components.	Results fully address all areas of importance to the organization's key requirements. Excellent trends and excellent performance are reported and strongly sustained in most areas relative to comparisons and benchmarks. Many areas demonstrate leadership.

Figure 6.3   Scoring guidelines
Taken from Baldrige Assessments, 1993–2000, NIST.

Feature	Scoring dimension	Maximum points	Maturity score	Weighted maturity score	Maturity level
Process governance	A/D	100	30%	30	
Performance metrics	A/D	75	30%	22.5	
POD/POA	A/D	50	20%	10	
Process capability and control	A/D	50	20%	10	
Process improvement	A/D	75	30%	22.5	
Process audit	A/D	50	0%	0	
Time management	A/D	50	30%	15	
Demand management	A/D	50	20%	10	
Cost management	A/D	50	50%	25	
Customer impact monitoring	A/D	100	40%	40	
Risk assessment	A/D	50	0%	0	
Supplier management	A/D	50	20%	10	
Customer results	R	100	30%	30	
Financial results	R	100	30%	30	
Process results	R	50	20%	10	
Total points		1,000		265	

Figure 6.4   PM³—Sample of an assessment scoring grid

process audit and risk assessment features show very little, if any, signs of activity.

This is all very nice, but how do you actually use it?

PM³: Application

The maturity model can be used in several ways and for different purposes. As a self-assessment tool, it is effective if the process team is engaged and gets involved by preparing well for the assessment exercise. Using a scoring board, colored dots, and flip charts, as well as a very able recorder, a skilled facilitator can do the exercise in one day. The process owner opens up the session with a brief update of recent accomplishments and the state of the process and explains the nature of the assessment.

The facilitator then explains the model and how the exercise will be conducted. Next each process feature is discussed, one by one. During the discussion, team members may appeal to data books or online databases and other material that help make a point. Afterward, the individual team members place their dots (marked with their initials) on the scoring board (shown in Figure 6.5). A discussion ensues to achieve

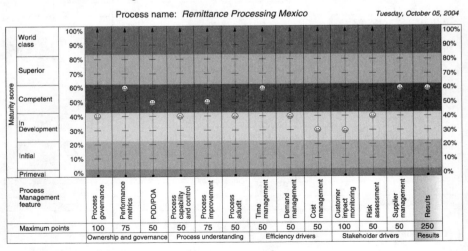

Figure 6.5   Scoring board

consensus on the score for the feature. The final score is simply a weighted score of all the features.

In addition to scores, which come naturally to managers in most of the organizations I've encountered, the self-assessment exercise also highlights strengths and weaknesses in order to come up with the scores. The team is encouraged to first discuss and understand the feature, then flush out strengths and weaknesses, and from these determine a score based on the guidelines. The mere act of discussing strengths and weaknesses is an important preamble to the "what do we do next?" question.

"We simply do not conduct periodic risk assessments of this process" becomes a significant weakness and an opportunity for improvement. If the opportunity turns into a project for building a risk management capability, then the score will improve. The real contribution, though, is that the end-to-end process is now better managed, with more control and less financial and legal exposure.

Again, the objective of the assessment is for the people, who work in the process and have a stake in it, to come to realize that there are very specific areas for improvement or strengths to amplify in making their process an excellent process. "Take it to the next level" now has an immediate, real, and visual impact—*"Next year, we go to the blue level."* (See Figure 6.6 for a schematic of the assessment process.)

Use of the maturity model makes the most sense when viewed dynamically. Once the assessment exercise is conducted, the team may

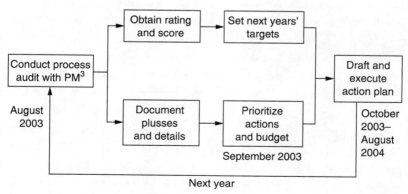

Figure 6.6 The assessment process

want to set a numerical assessment target for the following year or six months down the road. Simultaneously, the strengths and weaknesses are analyzed and prioritized: *"Yes, we have a lot to do . . . but what are the three to five initiatives that will address some of these issues and yet take us to the next level and make our process better?"* And an action plan and budget are drafted for the approval of the process owner. In nine to eighteen months another assessment is conducted to gauge progress.

Coda

PM^3 is but one of many process management maturity models in existence today, and probably, it's one of the more recent ones. Although several successful assessments have been done with this model, it is not stock and parcel of the wider AXP organization. Thus, its level of institutionalization is low, and its use can best be characterized today as optional and experimental. It isn't an end-all, either. Models need not be accurate, but they do have to be useful. Are they creating the sort of energy that organizations demand to foster change? We have to remind ourselves that in the enthusiasm of ownership or the joy in the act of creation, practitioners hang onto their ideas and long to put them into practice. Yet the marketplace of ideas is a very mixed bag of half-baked concoctions, ho-hum retreads, interesting concepts, and half a dozen gems. At some time, it may be well to realize, one's idea may fit in any of these categories.

Maturity models serve to spur organizations to higher levels of performance. They help to answer the question: "What's next?" And they provide management with assurances that a well-crafted, multigenerational plan is in place to foster excellence throughout the operation. They are probably of little use to low-performing organizations. As a consequence, one could make the case that maturity models are refinements, or one of the higher-order tools, in the process management toolkit.

The approach that Roberto describes should be a key component of many organizations' business process excellence journey. We believe that this approach, combined with periodic independent external assessments (such as Baldrige), provides an incredibly powerful means of determining progress and priorities on the business process excellence journey.

Closing Comments on Process Strategy,
and Some Words of Caution

We intentionally positioned *process strategy* between *process vision* and *process ownership* in our model for achieving business process excellence.

However, a process vision and strategy, coupled with a state-of-the-art approach for evaluating and improving process maturity (such as the one Roberto describes), is no substitute for a sound business strategy. The truth is, while business process excellence approaches such as Lean and Six Sigma can (and should) inform, shape, and guide an organization's business strategy, they are not, in and of themselves, a guarantee of business success.

A vision for the business should be the starting point for the development of any strategy.

To emphasize this point, a recent example from the United States should serve as a cautionary tale for us all. At Financial ServiceSolutions (FSS), a mortgage originations business, process outsourcing was established to provide people, process, and technology solutions for mortgage servicing. The organization was founded for a single purpose—to serve as a manufacturing utility for the mortgage industry, providing state-of-the-art mortgage service solutions. FSS proudly communicated that process excellence was a major strategic asset—in fact, it had even gone so far as to state, "Process Excellence is our Core Capability."[4]

Its approach to achieve world-class fulfillment was to link strategy with technology, business processes, and people, as shown in Figure 6.7.

Unfortunately, the demand for outsourcing mortgage refinancing significantly declined, and FSS was eventually closed down by the company's owners in April 2005.[5] Only time will tell whether this was caused by an ineffective business model, a poorly designed business strategy, bad luck, or a combination of these and other factors. What is clear is that even a commitment to world-class process excellence could not overcome those problems.

So, an organization's vision for its business, driving a sound strategy, executed through a robust business process excellence agenda that recognizes the value of the organization's processes as strategic assets, is the approach that organizations must take to achieve sustainable success.

Figure 6.7
Simply stated: the top priority at FSS is to remain client-focused at all times

In this chapter, we've seen how Bank of America uses the Hoshin-Kanri process to translate its vision into action. And we've seen how the Latin America region of American Express uses PM^3 to assess its process maturity in order to drive and execute a process-based strategy. In considering each of these organizations' progress with their Six Sigma efforts, it's difficult to imagine how they could have achieved their respective successes without such approaches.

In summary, it's not always a question of how visionary a leader is, but how well the leader can translate the vision into action—*strategy is, without doubt, execution!*

Notes

1. SixSigma Financial Services Ask the Expert, "The Topic: Six Sigma and Business Strategy."
2. Jim Buchanan, Quality and Productivity Transition Executive, *Bank of America IQPC Six Sigma for Financial Services* (July 28, 2004).
3. www.quality.nist.gov is the official Web site for the Malcolm Baldrige National Quality Award.
4. "The Path to World Class Loan Fulfilment—Dale Meder, Quality and Operations Executive, FINANCIALservicesolutions—Manufacturing Loans for the Mortgage Industry."
5. "FSS will lay off last of Louisville workers," *Louisville Courier-Journal*, February 18, 2005.

Establishing Ownership

I N THIS CHAPTER, we'll explain the importance of *process owner-ship* and describe how organizations can establish senior leadership ownership, cross-functional structures, and organizational accountabilities to achieve business process excellence results.

Many factors contribute to, and influence, a financial services organization's ability to successfully achieve business process excellence. We will focus on three key factors that leaders will need to personally address: clearly defining business process excellence roles and responsibilities, creating shared accountability for business process results, and leading change.

Clearly Define Roles and Responsibilities

A key responsibility in achieving business process excellence is to ensure that clearly defined *roles and responsibilities* exist within the organization to drive the effort forward.

While the specific role names may vary from organization to organization, many high-performing process-oriented financial services organizations establish formalized roles similar to the model team structure shown in Figure 7.1. These are likely to be different from the

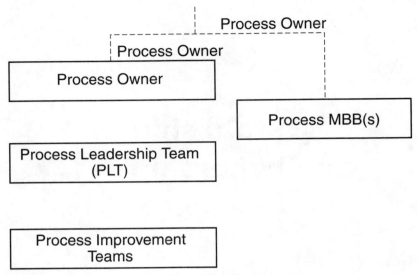

Figure 7.1   Process Ownership and Relationships

existing roles and responsibilities in the organization, so it is important that organizations take the time to ensure clarity and understanding.

The *process owners* should ideally be senior leaders who have ultimate accountability for each of their core end-to-end processes. As well, they should be members of the organization's senior management team, with a reporting line directly to the CEO or COO.

The key responsibility of process owners is to take personal ownership for leading the business process excellence effort across their assigned core end-to-end processes, and as such, they must:

- Establish and lead the cross-functional process leadership team
- Develop the process POA and multigenerational plan
- Regularly liaise with other process owners to ensure that end-to-end core process linkages and interfaces are understood and aligned
- Guide the business process excellence implementation
- Develop and establish process governance
- Make available required resources (e.g., resources for measurement planning and tracking)
- Support project teams, especially by removing barriers to cross-functional performance

- Be a role model—continually display and communicate the critical cross-functional behaviors required for business process excellence

Interestingly, it appears that this role is well understood by the financial services organizations we surveyed: They have all established an overall process owner for each of their end-to-end core processes, such as they're currently defined. It's also encouraging to see that in 36 percent of cases, this responsibility is with a member of the top senior leadership team. A member of the management immediately below the senior leadership team is responsible in a further 55 percent of organizations, and only in 10 percent of cases is a first-line manager in an operational or staff leadership position responsible.

The *process leadership team* should consist of senior functional managers representing all functions and external supplier organizations involved in the core end-to-end process. They are led by the process owner and should collaborate in a collegial manner to guide the business process excellence effort.

Actively led by the process owner, the process leadership teams typically have an evolving role. Initially, their key responsibilities are to:

- Participate in defining the process POA for the core process
- Establish the overall process architecture
- Identify resources for Green Belt and Black Belt training if required
- Provide resources for "infrastructure" efforts, e.g., voice-of-customer feedback, measurement systems, and process documentation
- Identify and approve Lean and Six Sigma projects
- Identify and manage conflicts with other project efforts such as IT initiatives that may be impacting their process
- Actively sponsor improvement projects and ensure transfer to control

As the business process excellence effort matures, this team's role evolves to support and sustain *process governance*, at which point the team's key responsibilities are to:

- Review process performance using the *Health of the Process dashboards*
- Monitor and guide the development of new scorecards and metrics
- Assess progress on closing data gaps
- Manage the *project portfolio:*
  - Identify and prioritize new improvement opportunities
  - Manage project conflicts
  - Assess progress on improvement plans
  - Conduct project tollgate reviews
  - Implement corrective actions
- Work with the enabling processes to optimize results such as *financial controls* and *IT support*
- Manage the change communication and engagement activities such as communicating the process POA, issuing regular updates on business process excellence, and providing details of project successes.

Although it's encouraging to see from our survey that cross-functional process leadership teams, reporting to the process owner, have been established in over 70 percent of the organizations surveyed, only 25 percent of these include internal business unit representation from across the *entire* end-to-end process. In fact, representation from both internal business units *and* external suppliers is taking place only in 25 percent of the organizations that have established a process leadership team.

Incidentally, in our experience many financial services organizations have well-established groups such as *quality councils;* in fact, some still remain from the days of total quality management. While these councils are responsible for much of the same actions as the process leadership team, they tend to be functional and may cover multiple processes. As financial services organizations transition to become more process oriented, the governance structure will need to change to ensure the right balance of functional and process reporting.

The Lean/Six Sigma Master Black Belts

The Lean/Six Sigma Master Black Belts should ideally be assigned to work with the process owner and the process leadership team for each end-to-end core process. As key contributing members of and participants in the process leadership team, their primary responsibilities are to:

- Operationalize the process POA by developing and syndicating a multigenerational plan
- Develop and execute end-to-end process measurement plans to ensure that robust dashboard data are available for decision making
- Support benchmarking initiatives
- Manage the end-to-end process project portfolio on a day-to-day basis
- Prepare updates for process review meetings
- Align and sequence Lean and Six Sigma projects for maximum impact
- Provide expertise in advanced improvement methods, tools, and techniques
- Facilitate Kaizen events and other breakthrough workshops
- Deliver Six Sigma training if not externally provided
- Conduct quarterly assessments of progress toward process maturity
- Provide day-to-day guidance to improvement teams

In Chapter 8, "Creating Capabilities," we discuss the role of employee certification in addition to providing more information on tools and techniques.

Improvement Teams

Improvement teams should be commissioned by the process leadership teams to address process transformation and improvement opportunities. Their key responsibilities are to:

- Refine Lean and Six Sigma project charters and validate the project rationale and value
- Select an appropriate improvement approach and level of investigation to develop effective solutions
- Maintain communication with the process leadership team
- Drive projects to successful completion

- Provide documentation of team efforts such as progress reports and project storyboards

Process Intellect Alone Is Not Enough!

Interestingly, while in our experience we've observed that many people working in financial services organizations understand the need for, and recognize the benefits of, boundaryless collaboration[1] at an *intellectual level*—after all, it's not in the same league as solving prime number theory—an *emotional disconnect* often exists that prevents those individuals, and therefore their organizations, from really getting these end-to-end process management components of business process excellence to *stick*. Consequently, these organizations fail to realize the enormous benefits that business process excellence approaches can offer.

Why is this the case, especially as the concepts are quite easily understood at an intellectual level? Actually, we think it's a very understandable human response, and it's consistent with one of the key questions that must be addressed for everyone involved in any change effort—"What's in it for me?" (WIIFM).

We shouldn't overlook the fact that organizations need the very people who are successful in the existing, often functionally oriented, organization to profoundly change the way in which the organization—and quite likely their performance—will be defined, measured, and managed. Is it any wonder that the natural human instinct is to resist such an approach!

To maximize business process excellence efforts, financial services organizations need to develop an intellectually robust approach *and* gain the acceptance and buy-in for the approach throughout the entire organization.

While there are many formulas and equations used in Lean and Six Sigma approaches for achieving business process excellence, we believe that this simple equation is the most important:

$$R = Q \times A$$

It shows us that results (R) are a function of the quality of our solution (Q) multiplied by the levels of acceptance (A) of that solution. So, for example, if we have the best possible solution in the world (a 10 out of 10), but we have little acceptance of it by the organization (1 out of 10), the results will be very limited indeed:

$$10 = 10 \times 1$$

However, if we focus our efforts more on increasing the organization's acceptance of our solution (5 out of 10), even at the expense of reducing the functionality of our solution (8 out of 10), the overall results we could expect to achieve would be significantly increased:

$$40 = 8 \times 5$$

In our experience, many financial services organizations relentlessly focus on the *quality of the solution* and fall short in achieving the required *acceptance* of their solution. Consequently their change efforts fail to achieve the results that are expected.

So how can organizations foster greater acceptance of solutions in order to truly achieve their business process excellence objectives?

Shared Accountability for Business Process Excellence Results

To ensure an execution and performance focus, today many financial services organizations establish clearly defined objectives and accountabilities for achieving results in a way that is relevant at a business unit level, a functional or departmental level, and an individual level. Many organizations utilize MBO (managing by objectives) approaches with formalized goal setting and review processes to ensure that the organization's vision and strategies are translated into meaningful and manageable goals[2] that can be understood and executed at all levels of the organization.

However, as we have previously described, these organizations are typically measuring and managing process performance on a function-by-function basis, as opposed to across their entire end-to-end processes. Similarly today, while many financial services organizations reward and recognize performance based on the results of the overall organization, at a personal performance level, it's highly likely that a large part of an employee's reward and recognition package is based on the results achieved by the function (e.g., finance, operations, sales) in which the employee works.

In fact, our survey findings indicate that reward and recognition today are almost exclusively functionally based (as opposed to core end-to-end process based) in over 80 percent of financial services organizations. In only less than 10 percent of the organizations surveyed is a percentage of an individual's compensation based on end-to-end process performance—the actual performance that customers experience!

In our view, such an approach fails to focus employees' actions and behaviors on the end customers' process experiences and perpetuates a functional (silo-based) focus—in many cases, at the expense of the end customers. This situation appears to be endemic in numerous financial services organizations.

An Alternative Way

If organizations are truly serious about achieving business process excellence, an alternative approach to managing performance is required. In our experience, the key question that needs to be addressed for people in any change situation is, as noted earlier, "What's in it for me?" (WIIFM). If they don't see a compelling reason to change, they won't. It's a simple, although at times unsavory, fact that people generally need to be given incentives to demonstrate and adopt new behaviors—and for many people in financial services organizations, cross-functional behaviors will be new.

We've seen a number of organizations that have attempted to create these new cross-functional behaviors by changing things around on their organization charts. While this is one approach that may work from time to time, we would *not* recommend such an approach for the simple reason that the scope of the change required often severely impacts the business; in fact, in some cases it will bring it to a complete standstill. What's more, despite messages that leaders may communicate to their organization about the reasons for making such changes (e.g., to achieve a stronger *external* focus), the change process in itself will actually create a very large *internal* focus as people try to figure out the organizational implications for them—WIIFM.

While it's possible that business process excellence initiatives *may* necessitate some organizational changes down the road, the best approach that most organizations can take at the start of their business process excellence effort is to find subtler ways to create a shared, cross-functional sense of accountability for their end-to-end processes. This is often best done by leveraging existing well-established approaches such as the organization's annual goal-setting and review process.

Given the prevailing WIIFM mindset, the approach we highly recommend is to use performance-related pay (bonuses) as a means to initially motivate and instill cross-functional behaviors, and a key component that should be used to drive the performance-related pay is the *Health of the Process scorecard*. This approach applies equally to your management of third-party suppliers who participate in the process supply chain. The Health of the Process scorecard should be an integral component of your commercial contract and service-level agreements with these partners. We'll explore this topic further in Chapter 10.

In the example in Box 7.1, a number of components are used to determine an individual's performance-related pay. The key difference with the implementation of the business process excellence approach is that the bonuses individuals receive are no longer based on the performance of their function (e.g., finance, operations), but instead based on the performance of the cross-functional end-to-end processes that the organization's customers actually experience—what a concept!

This approach fosters, recognizes, and rewards the cross-functional behaviors that are critical to achieve business process excellence. We call it the "Three Musketeers" approach—"One for all, and all for

Box 7.1

	Before BPE	With BPE
Drivers of Performance-Related Pay:		
• Overall organization performance	20%	20%
• End-to-end process performance	0%	40%
• Function performance	50%	10%
• Individual performance	30%	30%

one!"[3] In other words, the process participants within an end-to-end process either all succeed or all fail together, depending on the extent to which the end-to-end business process excellence vision and objectives are met.

This is a critical component of an organization's business process excellence approach, without which the required cross-functional behaviors are highly unlikely to materialize. For many, it's also one of the most challenging aspects of their business process excellence journey.

There's no better message the process owner and process leadership team can send their respective organizations than committing to such an approach themselves at the very start of their business process excellence journey!

Closing Comments on Part 2

To realize the benefits that business process excellence can create for financial services organizations, truly outstanding leadership courage, commitment, tenacity, and vision are required. The business process excellence journeys that organizations are now required to make are not for the fainthearted, and for many it will take them to new and as yet unexplored worlds:

> *Leading from good-to-great does not mean coming up with the answers and then motivating everyone to follow your messianic vision. It means having the humility to grasp the fact that you do not yet understand enough to have the answers and then to **ask the questions** that will lead to the best possible insights.*[4]

Those leaders and organizations that have both the maturity and humility to acknowledge that they don't have all the answers at the start of their journey will stand the greatest chances of ultimate success.

Achieving business process excellence is not a program—it's a philosophy; it's a way of life; it's a journey that never ends. And experience has shown, it's not a journey that can be successfully completed by all who start it. The business process excellence journey—whether with a Six Sigma, Lean, or BPM focus—is now one that all organizations must take if they want to successfully compete and create sustainable value in the long term.

Notes

1. *Boundaryless Collaboration* is a term regularly used by Jack Welch to describe cross-functional performance and behaviors.
2. Organizations often using SMART—*specific, measurable, attainable, relevant,* and *time-bound.*
3. With our sincerest apologies to Alexandre Dumas.
4. Jim Collins, *Good to Great* (New York: Random House, 2001).

3

Process Knowledge

Terrain gives birth to measurement.
—Sun-Tzu, The Art of War[1]

Introduction

In Part 2 we introduced our business process excellence model and addressed the Process Leadership component, the first of the three critical components required to achieve business process excellence. In Part 3 of our book we will address the second component, Process Knowledge, which comprises process capabilities, process architecture, and process measurement (see Figure P3.1.)

Just as generals in battle, today's financial services executives must understand their terrain. Once leaders recognize the value of a process-based organization, their next step is to understand and measure the

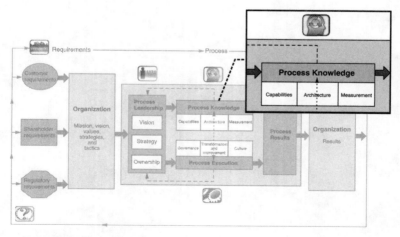

Figure P3.1

terrain or process(es). We have organized our thinking on this topic into three areas of knowledge that business process excellence leaders will require.

> First, leaders must understand how well prepared their resources are for achieving business process excellence. Does the organization have the knowledge and skills (i.e., *process capabilities*) to "make it happen"?
>
> Second, leaders must understand their processes and how they interact or fit together to create value. This is called *process architecture*. This is an organization's terrain.
>
> Third, leaders must understand the strengths and weaknesses of their processes. This is achieved through *process measurement*.

Notes

1. Ralph D. Sawyer, *Sun Tzu—The Art of War* (New York: Barnes & Noble, 1994).

CHAPTER

8

Creating Capabilities

In THIS CHAPTER, we'll focus on the importance of process capabilities and describe how leading financial services organizations are going about developing the capabilities they need to enable their business process excellence efforts to succeed. So what are the process capabilities that financial services organizations need to establish in support of their business process excellence efforts?

Pete Pande, president of Pivotal Resources, a global change leadership consulting firm, and lead author of *The Six Sigma Way*,[1] explains that typically in working with organizations, clients express a need for a variety of capabilities to be developed. Depending upon the business improvement objectives the organization has established, these can include:

- Developing awareness of the impact that process management, Six Sigma, and Lean methodologies can have on strategic, financial, and other corporate goals
- Understanding how to lead a sustained effort and drive a results-focused vision
- Creating or refining performance metrics to enable ongoing process control and the identification of critical gaps and improvement opportunities

- Standardizing the process of identifying and selecting improvement projects based on strategic impact, financial return, or other key criteria
- Ensuring that the right people are selected to perform the roles of project leaders, project team members, and project champions
- Identifying and prioritizing projects and supporting project teams
- Instituting the DMAIC problem-solving model and other process improvement methods such as Lean, FastTrack/Kaizen, and DMADV
- Providing project coaching to reinforce capabilities and drive project results
- Building a critical mass of knowledge within the organization to ensure that Lean Six Sigma methods and skills are sustained
- Measuring the ongoing success of the initiative and planning activities to drive future results

The approach to establishing these capabilities within an organization is often a combination of consulting, training, coaching, mentoring, and certification—typically involving orientation, strategy development, project preparation, launch and roll-out, and integration and sustaining activities throughout the entire deployment life-cycle.

Since the early days of Six Sigma, many organizations have chanted the mantra of inculcating Six Sigma knowledge into the leadership of their organizations, and various approaches have been taken to achieve this.

Something we often hear from leaders is, "We've got to standardize work and make sure every associate understands how his or her individual performance contributes to quality process output. We've got to get every associate thinking lean and capable of basic root cause analysis."

This is all well and good, but such an approach alone will not transform a business. It's actually the behaviors of the leaders themselves that need to change in order to transform a business and deliver sustainable improvements. We believe this is the single most immediate and critical challenge for organizations today—how to change the mindsets and behaviors of leaders to ensure that the concepts and principles of Lean and Six Sigma are fully integrated into *their* everyday thought processes and decision making.[2]

It must be remembered that capabilities building takes time—it's not just about training. New capabilities are established through a combination of just-in-time training, application, reflection, and internalization. Such an approach will yield results, but it requires time.

Under Jack Welch's leadership, GE indisputably led the Six Sigma charge throughout the mid to late 1990s. The organization launched its highly documented Six Sigma journey in 1995 with an initial focus on improving productivity. In 1997 the emphasis shifted to product design, and in 1999 GE implemented its "At the Customer for the Customer" (ACFC) program.

By 2001, Six Sigma had become firmly interwoven into the ways in which the organization worked. GE started focusing more on developing its future Six Sigma leaders and established a common organizationwide training and certification approach. Six Sigma leadership capabilities and experience became, and remain to this day, critical credentials for upward career progression at the company.

GE recognizes that the experience their employees gain from working on Six Sigma projects enable its future leaders *to build their process thinking* capabilities and *to understand the value of using data to drive decisions from an outside-in perspective*—two of the key skills that its people must demonstrate to progress within the organization.

Today, GE continues to increase the percentage of its senior leadership jobs going to former Master Black Belts and Black Belts—*all* employees are required to attend training and are subsequently tested. What's more, Green Belts can be certified following training and testing only if they're able to demonstrate tangible improvements to the organization's key Y (output) business process metrics, from their projects. Without doubt, Six Sigma is truly embedded in GE's organizational DNA and continues to further evolve.

While Merrill Lynch started its Six Sigma efforts some time after GE, it too understands the value of having its leadership fully skilled in Six Sigma. At this organization, "The goal is not only to give the company's future business leaders Six Sigma expertise, but also to ensure that the Six Sigma program develops better business leaders."[3]

In our survey of financial services organizations, we asked about the need for employees to demonstrate success in Six Sigma or Lean application to achieve career progress. Interestingly, 64 percent of organizations responded that this can be a prerequisite to career progress, although it varies by position.

On a related point, our survey also indicated that 70 percent of organizations require their business transformation initiatives to utilize specific methods, tools, and techniques, which is undoubtedly driving the growth of Six Sigma and Lean project capabilities. This may well support the commonly held view that business leaders who have achieved a specific level of certification such as Lean Expert, Green Belt, Black Belt, or Master Black Belt are, in turn, requiring their organizations to use these same methods, as they've learned firsthand the value such approaches can deliver.

In addition, we are increasingly seeing anecdotal evidence of financial services organizations describing Lean and/or Six Sigma skills and experience as "preferred" in their job postings. By simply visiting the career opportunities pages on most financial services organizations' Web sites and entering the words "Six Sigma" in the search field (not the job title field), you will often find hits. While this samples only current job openings, it nevertheless demonstrates the growth in this skill as a requirement for hiring. Over time, we fully expect to see many more organizations adopting, adapting, and emulating the approaches GE initially pioneered as they create business process excellence capabilities and competencies within their own organizations.

However, a focus on establishing Six Sigma capabilities in an organization from the bottom up can create significant employee demand for training, which, in itself, can create challenges for organizations. On the one hand, financial services organizations clearly need to develop new, leading-edge capabilities in methods such as Six Sigma, Lean, and Business Process Management to compete successfully. On the other hand, experts in adult education methods counsel that training is most effective when it offers the opportunity for just-in-time application, and from an organization's perspective this really should be on a specific and real business opportunity.

In attempting to achieve momentum, organizations have to carefully balance their need to achieve critical mass in the new capabilities they require with the need to ensure that the training provided is in response to a real business requirement. We've seen a number of organizations learn this lesson the hard and expensive way.

For example, a common error that is often made at the start of Six Sigma deployments is to provide some form of class-based "awareness" training to all employees, without any real opportunities for immediate and continual application of these newly learned skills. This is often highly demotivating for employees, and ultimately it is of questionable value to the organization, especially in organizations that have failed in previous attempts to deploy business improvement initiatives (such as corporatewide quality programs).

DBS

Over the last five years, the Development Bank of Singapore has been pursuing a large-scale business process transformation program. During this time, it has learned a number of key things[4] about training that we believe are of value to any organization embarking upon a similar effort:

- One size can't fit all.
- Be flexible with the programs. Customize them for the situation.
- Have a judicious mix of mass and just-in-time training
- Utilize e-learning to reduce course duration; it increases and accelerates coverage and provides an easy-access "refresher" course.
- Track and measure "engagement" to ensure value from the training.

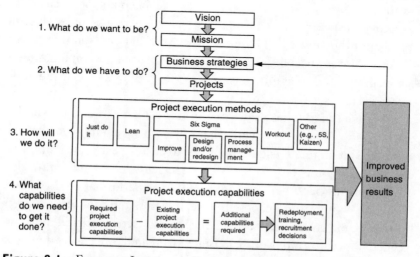

Figure 8.1 European Investment Bank deployment and capabilities model

An approach that's being taken at a second-tier European investment bank to ensure that capabilities are being established in response to specific business needs is shown in Figure 8.1. This deployment model enables the bank to ensure that the projects its employees work on have strategic relevance and that they are creating new operational capabilities in response to a specific business demand, thereby maximizing the return on their capabilities-building investment.

To Certify or Not to Certify—That Is the Question

The subject of *certification* is a difficult one for many organizations, and there are pros and cons to be considered. The main argument in favor of certification is that it offers a way of formally recognizing demonstrated capabilities and employees' contributions (namely, project successes) and that it can be part of a clearly defined developmental path (Green Belt to Black Belt to Master Black Belt).

The main arguments against certification are, first that there's no common and widely recognized standard.[5] Being certified as a Black Belt in one organization could mean and require something completely different in another organization. It can also perpetuate a perception that Six Sigma resources are part of a secret and exclusive *"priesthood."* Second, a certification program is often time consuming to administer. Last, and perhaps the most important, argument against certification is that employees can become too focused on meeting certification requirements at the expense of delivering results for the business. Those organizations that do decide to certify their employees take different approaches involving a combination of written and oral examinations and project reviews—again no standards exist.

While it's hard to take sides on this critical issue, it's important that each organization first evaluate what it wants to accomplish with certification. Is it merely recognition or is it to ensure that those employees the organization is entrusting as change agents have a minimum skill level that has been demonstrated by actual performance? Whatever direction organizations choose to take, it is imperative to set the direction early and communicate it clearly. We have seen firsthand the unintended impact to employee dissatisfaction created by a poorly deployed and managed certification program.

A related issue that has begun to surface is how long should the training take and what content should be included. From our research, the average number of weeks of training for Black Belts, exclusive of Green Belt training or Six Sigma Design training, is between three and four weeks. Most organizations realize that not all tools are applicable in all situations; those who are going to be the key change agents, namely the Black Belts, must have the capability to decide when a tool is most applicable. This will only come from having a fundamental knowledge about each tool in their toolkit and when and how it should be used.

In our continuous effort to search for new and interesting program offerings, we have recently started to see classes advertised as Six Sigma for Financial Services, Financial Services Six Sigma, or Transactional Six Sigma. It is encouraging to see training focused with, hopefully, industry-specific applications and examples. On the other hand, the lack of a standard for the minimum program content may lead to fundamentally weak program offerings.

In the interview we held with Laura Currier from FESCo., a division of Fidelity Investments, we asked about the company's experience in training Black Belts and Green Belts and what key lessons they learned.

We had received consulting advice that "Transactional" Black Belts didn't need to know how to do hypothesis testing, Gauge R&R, or DOE. Early on, we made the decision that we wanted our Black Belts to be capable of going toe to toe with the best; we didn't want to provide "light" training. Our training is great; the BBs get excited about learning the stats tools—but I have to admit, we've yet to do more than a couple of projects in which we really needed to use all of the tools.

One of my big "a-has" was that it's the IMPROVE phase which is hardest. A Black Belt can prove beyond the shadow of a doubt that he/she has solved for $Y = f(X)$; that doesn't mean they'll be able to get people to change how they work. Since we're in the service business, we can't change settings on machines; we have to change people's behavior to get results. The good news was that we had learned a great deal about effective change management back in our re-engineering days; we had to dust it off and incorporate it heavily into our Black Belt and Green Belt training.

Our profile of what makes a successful Black Belt has evolved since we started. We used to stress analytical skills; now we talk about leadership, ability to build relationships and influence people. It's much easier to teach analysis tools to a natural change leader than teach change management to a data geek.

Sharpening the Saw[6]

A measure of the success of the adoption or acculturation of Lean, Six Sigma and BPM is the actual growth and evolution of the program itself. Our survey of financial services organizations found that 83 percent of respondents have a centralized group responsible for identifying new and leading-edge business improvement techniques and capabilities.

	Initiating 0 to 2 years	Developing 2 to 4 years	Sustaining 4 plus years
Leadership	• Externally driven primarily by consultants • A few key leaders in the organization are tasked with deployment responsibility • Uses one size fits all strategy • A few consistent goals are set, usually dollar targets for the overall organization	• Centrally driven by a corporate function • A centralized steering committee with business representatives begins to lead the deployment • Develops a core strategy; business unit-based goals set by a central group, customer goals begin to be introduced	• Organizationally balanced leadership between corporate and line functions • Local and process-based quality councils begin to assume responsibility • Each business adopts an individualized strategy based on their implementation maturity • Stretch or POA goals are set by business unit that links to overall strategy and customers's needs
Knowledge	• Utilize external MBBs to deliver training and assist in projects • Begins to define organizational process hierarchy • Limited measures of success, primarily dollar focused	• Central group leads some projects and assumes training responsibility • Initiates a process management program • Begin transition from functional metrics to high-level process metrics	• Project leadership assumed by the "business," training jointly supported • Process management program is well deployed • Process measures are in place and used by local councils to drive projects
Execution	• Limited benefit tracking • Organization begins to evaluate change impact • A new skill set and language begins to be adopted	• Central group assumes project and benefit tracking, often a project management office evolves • As training is internalized, it is adapted to the organizations' needs and cultures	• Line business assumes tracking and reporting • Tools and techniques are embedded in the way the organization does business • Culture drives changes through the use of their Lean Six Sigma program

Figure 8.2 Typical program phases of business implementation

This supports the contention that leading financial services organizations that have seen the value in deploying a Lean Six Sigma program have ensured that someone has responsibility for heading efforts to continually improve their process of knowledge development and deployment as well. Quite typically organizations begin by contracting with external Lean Six Sigma service providers and then shift to an internally led program as the organization matures and becomes increasingly experienced and self-sufficient.

Figure 8.2 shows the evolutionary phases of several of the critical dimensions that we have seen in successful deployments. Companies transition from using external expertise to adopting and adapting these programs to their culture.

At the same time there remain differences of opinion on what to measure to gauge the success of a Lean or Six Sigma deployment. For example, some organizations measure only the savings or revenue impact. Others track the number of trained employees. Others track a comprehensive array of measures such as sigma level improvement, project cycle time, or Black Belt productivity rates. Experience has shown that it is best to avoid reporting activity based measures such as training numbers without tying the results of each effort back to the investment made in capabilities building. As with all forms of performance measurement, the organization needs to first determine what's important and then establish the appropriate measurement system to incent, drive, and reward the required behaviors.

Closing Comments on Process Capabilities

To truly succeed at business process excellence, financial services organizations will need to strengthen existing capabilities and establish new capabilities at *all* levels of the organization. As a leader, to simply approve training investments for junior-level resources on methods, tools, and techniques and then sit back and wait for good things to happen simply doesn't cut it.

Leaders need to start their capabilities-building effort by asking themselves some fundamental questions:

- How do we lead by example? What existing behaviors do we need to change, and which new behaviors do we need to exhibit?

- How do we build a continuous learning-doing-learning cycle into our organization to ensure that current and future leaders have the required process-oriented skills and experience?
- How do we value and recognize continual improvement in our business improvement knowledge development and delivery process?
- How do we determine capabilities-building requirements and match those to the appropriate levels of employees?
- How do we measure the success of our business process excellence efforts?

Ultimately, financial services organizations must become self-sufficient in their business process excellence capabilities. Anything less is a failure of leadership!

Notes

1. Peter Pande, Robert Neuman, and Roland Cavanagh, *Six Sigma Way: How GE, Motorola, and Other Top Companies Are Honing Their Performance* (New York: McGraw-Hill, 2000).
2. Patricia Collins, "Better Business Leaders," *iSixSigma Magazine* (September/October 2005).
3. How to achieve such a balance is fully explored in Peter S. Pande's *The Six Sigma Leader: Putting the Power of Business Excellence into Everything You Do* (New York: McGraw-Hill, 2006).
4. DBS, "The Transformation Bank," presentation made at the 2004 Asian Six Sigma Summit, (presenter unknown).
5. The American Society of Quality (ASQ) has a "body of knowledge" that is generally accepted as the closest to a common standard for Six Sigma Black Belt certification, although it has its origins in the tools required more in manufacturing environments than service and transactional environments
6. With thanks and apologies to Stephen Covey.

CHAPTER

Defining an Architecture

I N T H I S C H A P T E R, we'll concentrate on *process architecture* and recount how some leading financial services organizations are going about understanding their organization's end-to-end processes. For any organization striving to achieve business process excellence, the development of a customer-oriented process view of how the organization actually does things—we call this *process architecture*[1]—is a critical first step.

You might recall from our opening chapter that we defined a business process as "end-to-end work that creates customer value." In fact, "the difference between process and task is the difference between whole and part, between ends and means.... Customers care about results, and results are created by processes, not by disconnected individual tasks."[2]

Organizations, especially financial services organizations operating in highly regulated operating environments, have evolved in a very functionally oriented way and tend to be highly vertically integrated. There may have been, and may continue to be, very good reasons why this model is valid, but increasingly organizations need to cut through the functional boundaries that exist in order to understand and meet customers' requirements.

For many financial services organizations, establishing this "customer line of sight" through the organization may well be a new way of looking at their business. For others, it may be simply perceived as an extension of the Lean and Six Sigma approaches already being used, perhaps at a smaller-scale project level. However, the importance of process architecture cannot be understated. It provides the fundamental framework required to enable organizations to measure, manage, and optimize their business processes going forward.

Defining a Process Architecture

Process architecture can be described simply as the way all the individual processes fit together, just as the individual pieces in a jigsaw puzzle come together to create one image. As in a puzzle, it is often hard to see the big picture when looking at only the individual pieces. Most organizations establish their process architecture with different levels of hierarchy. This enables each process to be viewed within the context of the organization's overall "core" value-adding processes. A simple example is shown in Figure 9.1.

Any process begins with a request for a product or service by a customer and ends with delivery of that product or service to that cus-

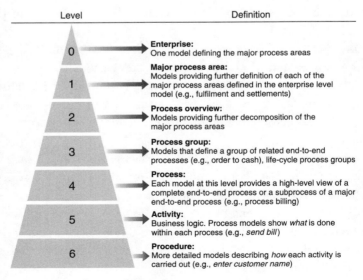

Level	Definition
0	**Enterprise:** One model defining the major process areas
1	**Major process area:** Models providing further definition of each of the major process areas defined in the enterprise level model (e.g., fulfilment and settlements)
2	**Process overview:** Models providing further decomposition of the major process areas
3	**Process group:** Models that define a group of related end-to-end processes (e.g., order to cash), life-cycle process groups
4	**Process:** Each model at this level provides a high-level view of a complete end-to-end process or a subprocess of a major end-to-end process (e.g., process billing)
5	**Activity:** Business logic. Process models show *what* is done within each process (e.g., *send bill*)
6	**Procedure:** More detailed models describing *how* each activity is carried out (e.g., *enter customer name*)

Figure 9.1 Process hierarchy tree

tomer. At an operational level, a *business process* can be thought of as a series of steps that are designed to produce the result for a customer. The process transforms *inputs* from *suppliers* into *outputs* for *customers* in a definable, repeatable, and measurable way. Although the need for such architecture may seem rather obvious, many financial services organizations do not yet appear to have a commonly held understanding of their processes. In our experience, we've found that if such process understanding and documentation exists at all, it's often in the hands of one group—typically IT—and is generally not well communicated, understood, accepted and, most importantly, *used* throughout the entire organization.

Interestingly, all the organizations we surveyed have started to define their core end-to-end processes at some level, with over 60 percent of respondents having commenced this work either at the enterprise level or within significant business units. However, at this point, only 10 percent have mapped and documented all their core end-to-end processes. A further 55 percent have completed this work for some of their core end-to-end processes, while remaining organizations are just beginning this work or are piloting the effort now.

Before we proceed further, we believe it might be helpful to provide some real-life process architecture examples. There are many terms and approaches in common use to gain such a perspective. In the absence of a set of standard predefined terms, we have chosen three high-level approaches that we labeled Lifecycle Relationship, Enterprise Activity Model (EAM), and Outside-In.

Life-Cycle Relationship Approach

We'll start with a very simple example from an organization that links its core business processes together in a way that mirrors its relationship with its customers throughout the relationship lifecycle.

This organization is a large U.S.-based financial services company with three major lines of business:

- *Electronic commerce.* Integrated electronic billing and payment services, available at more than a thousand financial services organizations such as banks, brokerages, and portals. In a typical quarter, 13 million consumers initiate online payments generating over 130 million transactions and receiving more than 22 million e-bills.

- *Investment services.* Portfolio management and reporting services, managing nearly 1.5 million portfolios totaling more than $900 billion in assets.
- *Software.* ACH Solutions, servicing over 66 percent of nations' 9 billion ACH payments; Financial & Compliance Solutions, providing reconciliation, financial messaging, work flow, and compliance software to more than 600 financial services organizations; and iSolutions, the leading provider of e-billing and e-statement software and services for B2C (business to consumer) and B2B (business to business).

The organization started its Six Sigma efforts in 1999 within its electronic commerce business, initially in one or two areas before broadening the deployment to other selective areas. Over the following years the company made good progress, and in 2003 it established a process enablement team within its electronic commerce business to support a fuller implementation. More recently, in 2004, it launched its companywide Six Sigma process excellence deployment supported by a newly created corporate process excellence team.

A key component of the organization's Six Sigma process excellence initiative is its enterprise level life-cycle relationship model. It

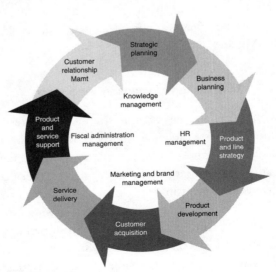

Figure 9.2 Enterprise level life-cycle relationship model

describes how activities across the business should be *organized*, relate, behave, and *work together* to deliver the organization's services to its customers and shareholders (see Figure 9.2). In fact, it's the basis on which the organization measures performance, diagnoses service issues, assesses and allocates improvement investment opportunities, manages process and procedural change, and drives accountability and achievement in all its services.

The organization's model is based upon a closed-loop customer relationship life-cycle approach, similar to that taken by many other organizations. It's a highly effective way in which to start establishing a process mindset within an organization from which more detailed-level process understanding can be developed.

Enterprise Activity Model

A somewhat different example is from Lloyds TSB, a major retail bank in the United Kingdom. We'll describe its story fully in Chapter 11 on process governance, as the bank has an excellent approach to share. For now, we'll simply introduce its enterprise activity model. It's the more typical kind of documentation used. As Figure 9.3 shows, the model essentially has five major activity areas:

You first 🐎 Lloyds TSB

1.0: Deliver sales and service
2.0: Manage customer relationships
3.0: Support the business
4.0: Direct and coordinate
5.0: Innovate the business

In total, these 5 major activity areas have 25 key subactivities, such as 1.1: Manage sales to customers and 5.2: Develop new channels. At the next level, these 25 key subactivities are composed of a further 85 lower-level activities such as 2.1.4: Refresh data and 3.2.2: Support the IT infrastructure. It's clear to see that process architecture can get big fast!

The approaches taken to creating process architecture at Lloyds are certainly very good ways to start to establish a process focus. However, these approaches are fundamentally an *inside-out* approach in the sense

1.0 DELIVER SALES AND SERVICE	2.0 MANAGE CUSTOMER RELATIONSHIPS	3.0 SUPPORT THE BUSINESS	4.0 DIRECT AND COORDINATE	5.0 INNOVATE THE BUSINESS
1.1 Manage Sales to Customers 1.1.1 Deliver product sales 1.1.2 Deliver registrations	**2.1 Manage customer information** 2.1.1 Develop holistic information requirements 2.1.2 Collect external data 2.1.3 Refresh data 2.1.4 Distribute data	**3.1 Provide and manage human resources** 3.1.1 Recruit 3.1.2 Train and develop staff 3.1.3 Remunerate staff 3.1.4 Provide personnel consumables 3.1.5 Motivate and communicate with staff 3.1.6 Dismiss staff	**4.1 Develop mission vision and values** 4.1.1 Develop and maintain mission 4.1.2 Develop and review strategy 4.1.3 Develop policies, values and culture 4.1.4 Develop procedures and rules	**5.1 Develop new products and services** 5.1.1 Adopt global proposition 5.1.2 Develop new propositions 5.1.3 Develop new products and services 5.1.4 Implement new products and services
1.2 Deliver transactions 1.2.1 Provide a money transmission service 1.2.2 Provide regular payments 1.2.3 Initiate and record transactions 1.2.4 Provide ancillary services 1.2.5 Process claims and maturities	**2.2 Develop customer insight** 2.2.1 Analyse data 2.2.2 Identify needs 2.2.3 Develop customer segment and treatments	**3.2 Provide and manage IT infrastructure** 3.2.1 Manage the IT infrastructure 3.2.2 Support the IT infrastructure 3.2.3 Manage software base	**4.2 Develop plans and budgets** 4.2.1 Produce and review plans 4.2.2 Translate plans into budgets	**5.2 Develop new channels** 5.2.1 Establish insights 5.2.2 Assess ideas 5.3.3 Establish business case 5.4.4 Develop channel 5.5.5 Implement channel
1.3 Change service 1.3.1 Process personal data changes 1.3.2 Process product data changes 1.3.3 Process transfers and closures 1.3.4 Process renewals 1.3.5 Replace lost and stolen cards	**2.3 Apply customer insight** 2.3.1 Determine contact strategy 2.3.2 Communicate to customers 2.3.3 Provide information to front line staff	**3.3 Provide and manage premises** 3.3.1 Acquire premises to requirements 3.3.2 Maintain and improve premises 3.3.3 Dispose of premises	**4.3 Control outcome vs plans and budgets** 4.3.1 Operate budgetary and financial control 4.3.2 Manage operational reporting review and control 4.3.3 Operate independent check	**5.3 Manage and coordinate change** 5.3.1 Identify need 5.3.2 Review and approve initiatives 5.3.3 Build change capability 5.3.4 Manage projects 5.3.5 Consolidate the learning
1.4 Manage information 1.4.1 Statement production and despatch 1.4.2 Manage enquiries and concerns	**2.4 Acquire new customers** 2.4.1 Identify target customers 2.4.2 Communicate to customers 2.4.3 Engage target customers 2.4.4 Establish customers 2.4.5 Reinforce the experience	**3.4 Provide procurement** 3.4.1 Manage procurement service 3.4.2 Provide customer consumables 3.4.3 Provide business consumables	**4.4 Manage internal and external communication** 4.4.1 Manage internal communication 4.4.2 Manage external communication 4.4.3 Provide representation on external bodies	**5.4 Provide knowledge management** 5.4.1 Set knowledge management policy 5.4.2 Collect and store information 5.4.3 Analyse information 5.4.4 Provide information to the business 5.4.5 Reinforce the learning
1.5 Control borrowing 1.5.1 Manage collections 1.5.2 Manage dept recoveries	**2.5 Build and maintain customer relationships** 2.5.1 Deliver CARE values 2.5.2 Manage customer feedback	**3.5 Manage financial assets and liabilities** 3.5.1 Match assets and liabilities 3.5.2 Manage cash to the network	**4.5 Manage risk** 4.5.1 Manage external relationships 4.5.2 Manage risk 4.5.3 Review and maintain adequacy of returns, ratios, etc.	**5.5 Build competitive capability**

Figure 9.3 Enterprise activity model

that the organization is really shaping its core processes from the perspective of what it does to address its customers' (and other key stakeholders') needs.

As we have seen, this approach typically identifies core processes or areas of activity such as:

- Developing new products and services
- Acquiring customers
- Processing customer transactions
- Processing remittances
- Servicing customers
- Handling customer inquiries
- Managing risk and prevent fraud

The Outside-In Approach

Another way in which financial services organizations can shape their end-to-end core processes is to take more of an *outside-in* approach.

This provides an even more powerful customer-driven approach to process architecture since it shapes an organization's core processes from the perspective of customers' experiences.

The process architecture continues to be based on a life-cycle perspective as before, but defines the processes from the customers' experience and perspective. So, for instance, rather than use language such as "acquire customers," organizations that adopt an outside-in approach might define the processes more in the way that customers would experience and view their interactions with the organization. For example, the language might be framed this way:

> As a customer, "*I* . . .
> apply for the product."
> use the product."
> pay for the product."
> upgrade the product."
> update my contact and financial details."
> get my inquiry or dispute resolved."

In shaping a financial services organization's core processes in this way, it's possible to create a framework that drives a much stronger customer-oriented way of process thinking, based on the customers' experiences.

We've found a single example of this approach from within a leading financial services organization.[3] Figure 9.4 depicts the approach. Note in the figure how this particular process architecture is organized around three key themes—inquire, buy, and use—and how each theme is preceded by a customer statement (e.g., *"I want something," "I make a decision," "I have a problem"*).

It's also important to note the distinction between *business partner/ external customer-facing processes* (shown at the top of Figure 9.4) and *enabling processes* and *supporting processes* (shown toward the bottom of the figure). *Business partner/external customer-facing processes* (often referred to as *core* processes) are those processes that directly create value and product movements. *Enabling processes* and *supporting processes* are those processes that, as their names suggest, *enable* and *support* value creation at the core process level.

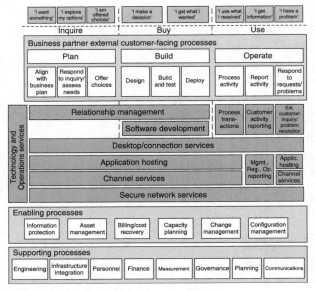

Figure 9.4 Outside-In Approach

Other Mapping-Based Approaches

Once the high-level components of the process architecture have been defined, syndicated with process participants, and agreed upon by senior leaders, the organization is ready to focus on the key components at the next level down in the process architecture hierarchy. The following approaches can be used both at enterprise and at the lower process levels, whereas the previous methods are primarily beneficial at the enterprise level only.

It is important to remember that the purpose of all hierarchy and mapping activities is to link the organization's process improvement activities to the enterprise model. Could you imagine a contractor building a house with only individual blueprints for each room and without a blueprint for the entire house that shows where the rooms go? Process architecture gives an organization a structure that enables everyone to better understand how work gets done.

Developing and documenting process architecture is *not* about mapping every single process of the organization to the nth degree. It's about establishing a process construct—starting at the highest level— as a basis for understanding those processes that create the most value for an organization's customers, shareholders, and other key stakeholders. If this isn't understood, it's difficult to comprehend how organizations can quantify the extent to which value is truly being created.

While it would seem there are further opportunities for focus in this area, many leaders who typically have the operating budgets to commission this kind of work often appear reluctant to do so—perhaps, in their earlier careers, they lived through an ISO9000 process mapping experience from hell!

Value Stream Mapping

As the business process excellence toolkit expands, organizations are increasingly leveraging combinations of Lean and Six Sigma techniques to address their process transformation and improvement opportunities. In fact, some financial services organizations are now starting to develop their high-level process architecture by applying value stream mapping (VSM) techniques that more typically have been used in manufacturing industries at an operational, plant-floor activity level. In our view, this is an extremely powerful approach and will increasingly be considered a "best-practice" developing process architecture. VSM has its own stylized language for documenting and communicating information about a process (see Figure 9.5).

While there are several approaches to value stream mapping that an organization can apply, the key concepts are the combination of process

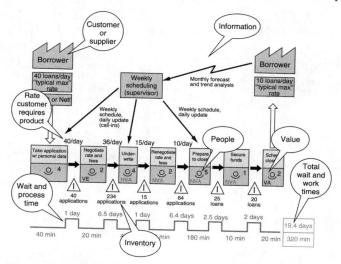

Figure 9.5 Value Stream Map (VSM) Example

data with the visual aspect of process flow. You would expect to see data such as processing time, cycle time value-added, and non-value-added time documented on a process diagram that also visually displays product, inventory, and information flow.[4]

The development of an organization's high-level process architecture is a critical starting point for creating a common understanding of how value is created for customers and other key stakeholders. It also provides a common process "language" and is a good approach for fostering a process-oriented culture within the organization.

SIPOC Mapping

Many organizations use a tool called a SIPOC diagram (SIPOC stands for *suppliers, inputs, process, outputs*, and *customers*) to create a bird's-eye

view of the process. SIPOC diagrams serve as very useful direction finders for identifying areas where further, more detailed process drill-downs are required.

The SIPOC diagram is a key Six Sigma tool and is now used widely within financial services organizations. Figure 9.6 presents an example

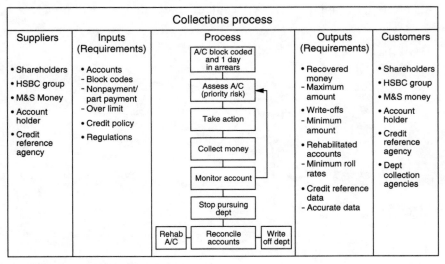

Figure 9.6 SIPOC diagram example

from Marks & Spencer Money, focusing on its credit card collections process (one of its eight enterprise-level end-to-end core processes).

While in many cases, SIPOC diagrams provide organizations with new insights on how activities are performed, they do have limitations, and so organizations typically use other tools such as process maps and value stream maps to understand how their processes operate at a more detailed level. We don't plan to get into this level of detail here.

Other Mapping Methods

There are several other common process mapping and flowcharting methods out there in use today, enough to fill an entire book! We have purposefully chosen not to cover these methods here because of most organizations' familiarity with those techniques.

Closing Comments on Process Architecture

In this part of the book we have transitioned from the high-level leadership view—the captain's view of the horizon the ship is trying to sail to—*to a view of the ship itself.* The ability of financial services organizations to understand their process architecture is the first step in understanding how the *ship* works and what the opportunities are for improvement.

Most organizations typically begin very tactically with project-based improvement initiatives, and as they achieve success and confidence with Lean Six Sigma methods and tools, their programs move more to higher-level process-based initiatives.

There are a few critical "take-aways" that we should note in closing this chapter:

1. *Value* in the process should be defined from the customer's perspective.
2. The process architecture is the critical foundation on which measurement systems and many other aspects of achieving business process excellence are based. It enables organizations to create a seamless connection from the customer, to the process, to

the measurement, to process improvements that benefit customers and shareholders.

3. The fundamentals of process leadership, vision, strategy, and ownership must be in place for the organization's efforts at process architecture to be truly successful.

4. The process architecture must be *actually used* in order to drive and accelerate change. Just mapping processes achieves very little. Processes need to be improved or transformed to realize value.

Just as process leadership is the foundation for architecture, architecture is the foundation for the development of an organizations' process measurement systems, which in turn become the foundation for the identification, prioritization, and successful execution of an organization's transformation and improvement efforts.

Notes

1. In some organizations this is referred to as an enterprise activity model or map.
2. Michael Hammer, "Business Processes in Financial Services," Microsoft white paper (September 2003).
3. Believed to be from Bank of America's technology and operations division, but source information is unavailable.
4. A recently published basic treatment of this topic can be found in the June 2006 issue of *Quality Progress* magazine. Unfortunately, as with so many of the best quality improvement tools, the examples are all manufacturing based.

Establishing Measurement Systems

Not everything that counts can be counted, and not everything that can be counted counts.

—Albert Einstein

IN THIS CHAPTER, we'll explain the importance of *process measurement systems* and discuss how some leading financial services organizations are going about implementing customer- and key stakeholder-driven measurement systems.

Data—and more importantly, data translated into meaningful and actionable information—constitute a critical requirement for *business process excellence*. Whether an organization is using Lean, Six Sigma, BPM, or a combination of approaches, the ability to continually measure and analyze performance is a prerequisite for transforming and improving the organization's processes to achieve and sustain optimal performance. Accurate, comprehensive, and key stakeholder-oriented measurement systems should be at the very heart of an organization's business process excellence efforts.

In our experience, financial services organizations typically find it very challenging to obtain the most fundamental and basic information about their end-to-end core processes—data such as unit cost and cycle time and, in some cases, even data as basic as total volume throughput. In the absence of this information, organizations are unable to optimize their performance using more sophisticated measurements such as rolled throughput yield, process capability, and process cycle efficiency. Consequently defects and waste exist throughout the organizations. This is even more challenging for many financial services organizations because defects and waste are not as easily visible as they are in a manufacturing facility.

However, this situation may be changing, and increasingly there's evidence to suggest that more and more leading financial services organizations use some form of performance scorecard to report and track their results. In fact, our survey findings indicate that just over 50 percent of respondents use some form of a *process-based* scorecard. Although they are not widely deployed, it is encouraging to see what we believe is a growing trend in the utilization of process-based scorecards.

Given the importance of such measurement systems not only for tracking and managing performance but also as a basis for identifying value-creating improvement and transformation opportunities, coupled with the *not* insignificant amount of time and resources typically required, this subject now appears to be a significant area of focus for many financial services organizations.

Regardless of the improvement methodologies an organization is using, the fundamental components required to establish a balanced set of key stakeholder-driven end-to-end measurements in support of business process excellence remain the same. Given an organization's process management maturity, the degree of emphasis may vary, although every organization, at some point, will need to:

- Establish a comprehensive, sophisticated, and diverse array of customer and process listening mechanisms
- Use a balanced scorecard for each core process containing leading and lagging indicators that are empirically linked to the ultimate drivers of customer behavior for that process
- Translate the balanced scorecard into a hierarchy of measures that are seamlessly linked across and up and down each core end-to-end process to facilitate performance management and problem solving
- Establish operational definitions for each measure and make sure they are commonly understood across the entire end-to-end process

- Operate a process for continually reviewing and assessing all measurements to ensure that the leading process indicators are correct

In our view a very simple and sometimes overlooked equation—shown in Figure 10.1—should form the foundation of any measurement system.

For many readers this equation will require no explanation; for others it might. So here's a short paragraph for those who would like an explanation.

We can think of the Y's as the *outputs* that customers and shareholders experience or receive from the process. For example, a customer's Y could be the receipt of a new credit card within seven days of making the application. A shareholder's Y could be the total value created from the process of managing credit card receivables. The important point to note is that the outputs are a function (f) of the X's, and so the degree to which an organization can achieve the customer's Y (i.e., receipt of a new credit card within seven days of making the application) is a function of the time it takes to execute the whole process.

It's also essential to note that not all X's are as important as others, and so organizations need to have measurement systems in place that enable them to identify the vital X's that have the biggest impact on each of the Y's. The most valuable measurement systems are those that enable organizations to predict the Y outputs based on close monitoring of their in-process X's. There are very few organizations that have

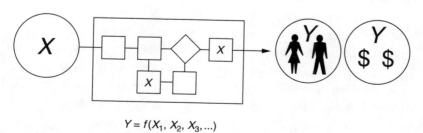

$$Y = f(X_1, X_2, X_3, \ldots)$$

Figure 10.1   An example of the relationship between outputs, process, and measures.
Reproduced with permission of Pivotal Resources.

achieved this level of measurement maturity for all of their core end-to-end processes.

One technical word of caution—the relationship between these measures must be verified quantitatively. While the process most organizations use to identify these measures generally begins with a combination of voice of the customer input and internal subject matter expertise, this is just the start. Creating a robust measurement system is one of the critical foundation blocks of Six Sigma, Lean, and BPM.

As the term *process measurement systems* suggests, the key foundation for developing measurement systems is a very good understanding of the organization's processes; note that without *process architecture*, it's likely that the wrong things will be measured. In those financial services organizations that are most advanced with their process excellence efforts, this understanding starts at the enterprise process level, where core end-to-end processes—the key value-creating processes of the organization—are defined. In less mature process-oriented organizations, the process understanding may exist at a lower level.

Once organizations have established a process perspective of how work gets done, they're able to start measuring how well it's currently done; that is, do the process outputs (Y's) meet the critical-to-quality requirements of customers and other key process stakeholders such as shareholders and regulators. To truly and constantly answer this question, organizations require a comprehensive, sophisticated, and diverse array of customer and process listening mechanisms that typically include many sources: surveys, focus groups, benchmarking, piloting, industry data, customer complaints (and compliments), lost customers, long-tenured customers, regulatory pressure, specific brand and process research, recommendations, and observations, to name a few!

Our survey findings suggest that the concept of establishing a process measurement system that detects and communicates how well an organization is meeting customers' needs and expectations remains relatively new in the financial services industry, with less than 20 percent of respondents having established such a system. So, overall our survey findings suggest that while some encouraging steps are now being taken by a number of leading financial services organizations, there's clearly a very long way to go in respect to this business process excellence requirement.

Citibank—a member of Citigroup—has introduced a customer information approach[1] that could quite possibly be the envy of many financial services organizations. The approach is  structured around three key areas of focus, covering the entire customer lifetime relationship with the organization: customer innovation, customer intimacy, and customer listening posts. The customer intimacy and customer listening approaches are particularly interesting and relevant at this point.

Citibank's approach to customer intimacy within its corporate banking division involves:

- *Customer blending.* An approach in which customers are integrated into the organization itself in order to cocreate solutions.
- *Needs group.* A group established to anticipate emerging needs for a specific customer population.
- *Customer ecosystem mapping.* A technique for exploring ways in which products and services can be expanded throughout the customer's value chain.

Within the bank's retail division, customer listening posts provide additional and multiple perspectives on customers' experiences and requirements through the use of:

- *Relationship-based surveys.* Focusing on gaining insights from key decision makers through in-depth interviews.
- *Transaction-based surveys.* Offering perspectives from final product users (as opposed to decision makers) on specific operational details.
- *Customer touch points (such as CitiPhone).* Enabling the capture, compilation, and analysis of customer-initiated contact.

This array of approaches allows Citibank to continually close the knowledge gaps it has in terms of customers' product and process experience requirements. On the basis of this understanding, Citibank is able to develop the appropriate measurement systems to track and report its product and process performance. A simple example of how

Citigroup has created actionable metrics, aligned to the key drivers of customer satisfaction for ATM cash access, is shown in Figure 10.2.

Organizations taking an approach similar to Citibank's soon learn that there are potentially a lot of things they can measure, and so they find it's very important to establish a *balanced scorecard* for each core end-to-end process containing a combination of the *vital few* indicators. With so many possible measurements to choose from, the challenge at this point for many financial services organizations using Six Sigma, Lean, or any other approaches to achieve business process excellence is to decide on what to include in their balanced scorecards.

Typically, organizations have based their reporting on output indicators (Y's) that for the most part are lagging indicators, good examples being financial indicators such as those found on profit and loss statements or customer satisfaction scores. The concern with relying on only these types of measurements is that they're essentially providing a still picture, published *after* the event, documenting what happened.

To compete successfully in a dynamic global operating environment, financial services organizations need to have significantly more advanced measurement systems, ones that more resemble real-time

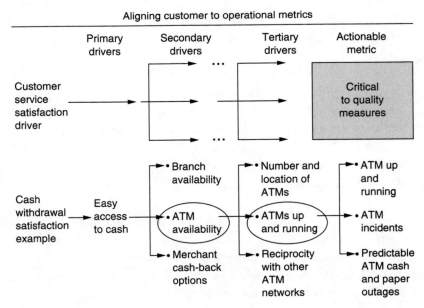

Figure 10.2

video streaming over the Web than a still photo. These should contain, for example, leading indicators—similar to those used in brokerage operations—to predict performance, thereby enabling process participants to proactively take actions to influence and control the process outputs.

Over the last few years, the use of Six Sigma and Lean measurement techniques has significantly enhanced the original concepts of balanced scorecards. Today, the scorecards used will most likely contain a diverse array of measures—leading and lagging, financial and product, efficiency and effectiveness, output and process, and external customer satisfaction—that enable organizations to make significantly better informed decisions than in the past. (See Figure 10.3.) These core end-to-end process dashboards, constructed using balanced scorecard concepts and sometimes referred to as *Health of the Process* dashboards, are an integral component of any organization's business process excellence journey.[2]

The example *Health of the Process* scorecard shown in Figure 10.4 is from UBS, a leading global investment bank. As part of the bank's Process Excellence program in its Investment Banking operations, it is establishing similar dashboards (the term it prefers to use for this kind of report.)[3] in response to a set of highly focused stakeholder requirements.

Note the use of graphics, the simplicity of design, and the overall visual impact.

Efficiency	Effectiveness
• Total cost	• On-time delivery
• Total cycle time	• Adherence to specs
• Resources consumed	• Service experience
• Amount of rework	• Accuracy
• Cost of defects	• Value-added features
• Scrap or waste	• Customer satisfaction

Figure 10.3
Reproduced with permission of Pivotal Resources.

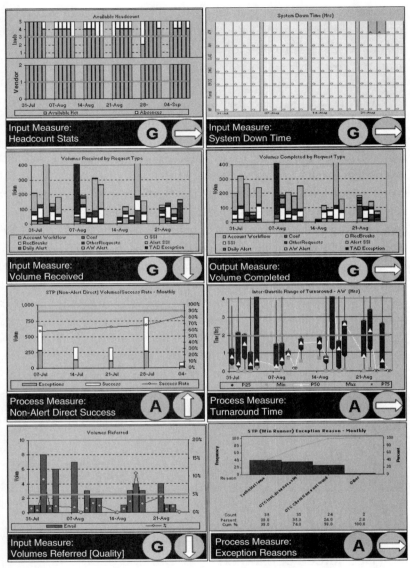

Figure 10.4 An example of a "Health of the Process" scorecard

To enable the *Health of the Process* scorecards to be used by organizations as a means to identify specific defects—the starting point for transformation and improvement efforts—a clearly defined and carefully constructed measurement hierarchy is required. In addition, this is a vital component to ensure that performance on each of the key dashboard metrics can be both rolled up and decomposed throughout all levels of an organization's process architecture.

Creating a Hierarchy of Measures

A measurement hierarchy enables organizations to seamlessly link the metrics contained within their balanced scorecards both across and up and down the end-to-end process. As we described in the previous chapter on process architecture, each core and enabling process will have its own subprocesses, each of which can be further decomposed into subprocesses, and so on. This same hierarchical process architecture can and should be used to structure an organization's measurement hierarchy.

One specific question that many organizations raise when creating measurement hierarchies is whether the linkages should be created in a top-down or bottom-up way. While it's often quicker to establish a high-level process scorecard than a lower-level one due to less detail being required, this can cause some issues. The key challenge in taking a top-down approach is that organizations are unlikely to know the drivers of those measures and the strength of the relationships; consequently, they may identify measures based on intuition and guesswork, with little or no relationship to the true drivers of process performance.

The benefit of taking a hierarchical structure to measurement is that it ensures the measures being developed are completely aligned with the processes within the organization. It also allows organizations to create process reporting that's relevant to each level of the process leadership throughout the process.

As measures are identified, it's extremely important to create clear operational definitions to ensure the measure is commonly understood across the entire end-to-end process and to enable accurate data collection. In the absence of this critical documentation, it's extremely likely that process participants will collect different data based on their best guess of what's required. This will, of course, severely compromise the organization's ability to track performance, identify improvement opportunities, and compare performance across units.

An example of a high-level measurement framework for a merchant statement process is shown in Figure 10.5. Note the measurement *tier,*

Process	Tier	Measurement type	Metric	Operational definition
Statementing	1	Cost	Statement cost per active merchant ($)	The total statement cost as per Ledger 3759 divided by the total number of active merchants as per activity report 4862
	2	Volumetric	Statements issued (#)	The total number of statements issued as per report 7899
	3	Volumetric	Merchants on monthly statement (%)	The total number of merchants receiving monthly statements as a percentage of the total number of merchants receiving statements
	3	Volumetric	Electronic statements issued (%)	The total number of electronic statements as a percentage of the total statements issued
	2	Cost	Unit cost per statement issued ($)	The total statement cost as per Ledger 3759 divided by the total number of statements issued as per report 7899
	2	Cycle time	Statement issued on time (%)	The total number of statements issued on time divided by the total number of statements issued as per report 7899
	2	Accuracy	Total reconciliation process-related inquiries (#)	The total number of financial inquiries (mail and telephone) as a percentage of the total incoming volume. Discount rate questioned, discount rate rebates, debit balance inquiry, reconciliation.
	2	Customer satisfaction	Merchant satisfaction (gap vs. competition) with reconciliation process (%)	The gap between the average merchant satisfaction rating with the company reconciliation process, and the average merchant satisfaction rating with the lead competitor's reconciliation process

Figure 10.5 Measurement framework example

showing the hierarchical relationships between the measures; the different measurement *types:* cost, volume, cycle time, accuracy, and customer satisfaction; and the detailed *operational definitions.*

On a final note, measurement is a journey, not a destination. The more organizations learn about their processes, the more they may want to measure. Some measures that are critical to organizations today may be less important next year as business demands change or new and better measures are identified and introduced. Organizations that fully understand measurement concepts build the continuous review, development, and refinement of their measurement systems into their Lean, Six Sigma, or BPM deployment programs. But creating such systems can be expensive. One practical approach that a number of financial services organizations take is to allocate a percentage of their ROQ (return on quality— i.e., the savings or value created by their Lean Six Sigma initiatives) to improve their measurement systems.

Closing Comments on Process Measurement Systems

Organizations need to measure performance constantly and intelligently *and* analyze that performance across a comprehensive range of dimensions. An inability to do this prevents financial services organizations from managing and continually optimizing their performance. Increasingly, financial services organizations are recognizing that their monolithic, lagging indicator–oriented measurement and management information systems require significant overhaul and redesign to enable them to understand the fast-changing requirements of customers in the highly dynamic and competitive marketplaces in which they are operating.

There's now an increasing use of real-time digitalized approaches to ensure that process leaders and participants always have up-to-date operational performance data at their fingertips, approaches similar to the kinds of information systems and analytical tools widely used in investment brokerage operations where value can be realized and lost in an instant. However, there is also sufficient evidence to suggest that the approaches being taken by many financial services organizations to measurement systems will significantly constrain their business process excellence efforts. As a result, these organizations may be in an ultimately untenable position as they will increasingly fail to meet customers' requirements, and in doing so, will fail to optimize their returns to shareholders. In an industry characterized and engendered by consolidation and rationalization, these organizations had better watch out.

Notes

1. Alexis Goncalves, Director—Global Quality Intelligence, "Amplifying VOC through Innovation," Citigroup Global Consumer Bank, Six Sigma for Financial Services Conference, New York (July 27–28, 2004).
2. *Health of the Process dashboards* are essential tools that can be used at *process review* meetings to determine performance and progress toward the end-to-end process point of arrival (POA). We'll describe the process review meetings and the way in which the scorecard approach is being used to achieve business process excellence by one major U.K. retail bank in the next chapter.
3. *Author's comment on terminology:* We have found a lack of consistency among the companies we surveyed in their use of the terms dashboard and scorecard. Some have stated that the dashboard is high level and more graphical, while the scorecard is more detailed and lower level in nature, but even here the application was inconsistent. Our recommendation is to establish a common definition for your organization and attempt to stick to that terminology in all your communications.

4

Process
Execution

Introduction

In Part 4 we will introduce the final component of our business process excellence model—Process Execution. This component covers three key "how-to" topics:

- How to manage an end-to-end process
- How to apply Six Sigma, Lean, and process management project methods, tools, and techniques to transform and continually improve the business

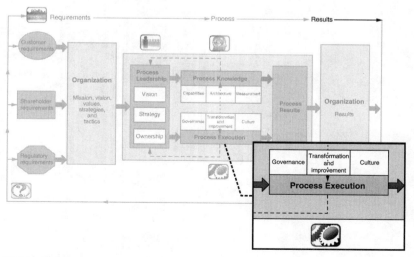

Figure P4.1

- How to foster a culture that recognizes, values, and rewards these capabilities

Finally and most importantly, as we have done in previous chapters, we share examples of how leading financial services firms are doing these things today—in the real world.

Embedding Governance

I N T H I S C H A P T E R, we'll detail the importance of *process governance* and describe how some leading financial services organizations are going about establishing end-to-end process governance as part of their approach to achieving business process excellence.

Exploring Process Governance

As we described earlier, the role of the process leadership team is unlikely to be fixed throughout an organization's business process excellence journey. It typically changes and evolves over time.

Initially the process leadership team's role is to introduce and establish the critical business process excellence components such as process dashboards and measurement systems. Once these enabling requirements are established, the process leadership team's focus will increasingly evolve to one of *process governance*, using the business process excellence infrastructure to successfully manage, transform, and improve the organization's processes.

So what specifically do we mean by *process governance?* Today, as a leader managing a department—or, indeed, a process—it's likely that you will need to understand a number of basic things. For example, you will need to know how work activities get performed and who does them; you will need data and information to quantify performance; you will need to set goals and establish accountabilities so that we can recognize and reward performance; you will need to motivate people and foster an environment that strives for continual improvement and success; you will need to deploy people to the highest priorities.

In this sense, *process governance* is no different from the process of managing a function such as operations or sales. The key challenge—and, of course, the big difference—is that in a process world, leaders need to understand these things from an end-to-end process perspective as opposed to the traditional function-by-function view of the world.

However, for many financial services organizations, it's often very difficult to gain a clear understanding of these performance characteristics because many organizations' information and performance management systems have been set up to mirror their existing functional or departmental operating constructs and procedures. As Michael Hammer observed:

> *High performance processes require new information systems. Fragmented processes are typically supported by equally fragmented departmental information systems, each of which employs its own database.*[1]

Regular Process Reviews

One of the key ways in which the momentum for a business process excellence effort can be maintained and further accelerated is through conducting regular *process reviews* as a central part of an organization's process governance approach. These core end-to-end process review meetings should be led by the process owner, who typically takes ownership for scheduling and, ideally, for chairing the meetings; note that initially it may be beneficial for the Master Black Belt designated to the process to take a facilitation role. The meetings will need to be very carefully planned and executed in order to maximize their impact and effectiveness.

Essentially, the purpose of the process review—at a minimum, generally held monthly—is to enable the process owner and the process leadership team to:

- Review process performance using the Health of the Process dashboard

- Assess overall process maturity and capability
- Monitor and guide the development of new scorecards and metrics
- Assess progress on closing data gaps
- Manage the *project portfolio:*
  - Identify and prioritize new improvement opportunities
  - Assess progress on improvement plans
  - Conduct *project tollgate reviews*
  - Implement corrective actions
  - Manage the change communication and engagement activities such as communicating the process POA, issuing regular updates on process performance, and reporting the details of project successes
  - Ensure that appropriate resources are assigned and actively engaged on all of the above

Our survey findings indicate that cross-functional process leadership teams have been established in over 70 percent of responding organizations. In 25 percent of cases, the majority of the team members are the top leaders of the organization. In addition, it's encouraging to see that 88 percent of the process leadership teams meet monthly; none of the teams meets weekly.

The agenda topics covered at the meetings include the following. The percentage of respondents whose process leadership teams cover each topic at their respective meetings is shown in parentheses.

- Resource discussions (100 percent)
- Process performance updates (88 percent)
- Project reviews (88 percent)
- Goal setting (75 percent)
- Deployment issues (62 percent)
- Process-based scorecard discussions (50 percent)

It's also particularly noteworthy, given the extensive reliance that financial services organizations have on IT systems for service delivery, that none of the respondent organizations, at this point, makes and evaluates technology investment decisions based on their impact on core end-to-end processes. There would appear to be opportunities for significantly improved value creation here based on a significantly improved technology investment evaluation and prioritization process that is better aligned with business priorities.

Throughout our research effort for this book, we have identified a few financial services organizations that have impressed us with their approach to process governance, but none more so than Lloyds TSB.

You first Lloyds TSB

In 2001, the retail bank at Lloyds TSB was keen to improve its customer service to gain maximum benefit from a number of major organizational changes the bank had made as part of its integration of financial services organizations such as Scottish Widows (a large life insurance company) and the Cheltenham & Gloucester building society (offering mortgages).

To support this, initially a number of "task forces" were set up to focus in on those processes that provided the most opportunity for improvement. Then, in 2002, a more formalized approach was established at the bank to ensure sustainable improvement going forward. At the heart of this new approach was a Process Owner Team (POT) framework that required the bank to look at its services on an end-to-end basis taking both customer and business perspectives into consideration.

Initially, 14 POTs were set up, covering all the bank's key retail customer-facing processes. The bank essentially developed a nine-step POT production process:

1. Agree on POT membership—ensure that members have the authority to act.
2. Agree on POT scope.
3. Appoint a process manager.
4. Bring stakeholders together in regular POT meetings.
5. Establish measurement and analyze.
6. Identify customer-centric critical success factors[2] and set targets.
7. Prioritize, prioritize, prioritize!
8. Develop actions plans and communicate to stakeholders.
9. Implement and manage plan to ensure delivery.

The POTs established end-to-end Sigma process measures and developed 36 "process dashboards" covering key retail customer-facing processes. By 2003 they were regularly monitoring and targeting improvements using these dashboards. At that time, the Sigma improvement methodology (Lloyds TSB's version of Six Sigma) was adopted to drive defect reduction and capture benefits.

The goal of process ownership at Lloyds TSB is to reduce defects, to improve customer service, and to drive down costs. Consequently, in order to achieve these objectives, the POTs have three key accountabilities in respect to their management of end-to-end processes: cross-functional collaborative decisions, actions, and prioritization.

Over the last few years, the bank has developed a number of automated tools to assist the POTs, and now it has an enviable management information system (MIS) to facilitate the process review meetings, providing such information as identified customer requirements, defined end-to-end process and standards, and identified movements in process performance (see Figure 11.1). In the first full year that the POTs were in place, first pass defects were reduced by 83 percent across 17 customer processes. On the basis of this impressive success, during the last few years, the bank has extended the approach across its entire group operations, and there are now more than 200 processes that are regularly reviewed by POTs. The bank is now integrating Lean

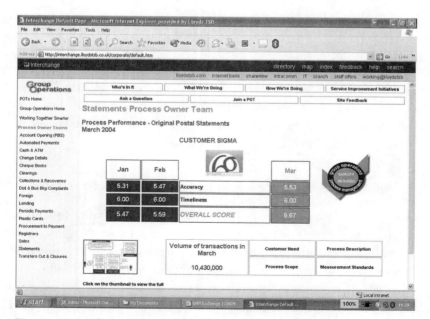

Figure 11.1 Process Operations Team—MIS

approaches into its Six Sigma and business process management approach to achieving business process excellence. It has learned the hard way and proved beyond doubt that managing processes end to end is not optional!

To return to the role of generic process leadership teams, in addition to the regular—typically monthly—process reviews that these teams will conduct, it's likely that they will also perform a number of tasks less frequently than the typical agenda items mentioned earlier—perhaps quarterly or annually. These include such discussions as:

- Reviewing progress against the process vision (POA)
- Evaluating process goals and objectives to ensure that the performance bar is set high enough
- Formally aligning process goals across all *process participants* as part of the annual performance management and planning process
- Establishing appropriate reward-and-recognition mechanisms to drive cross-functional, end-to-end behaviors
- Inviting external process constituents (suppliers and partners) to participate in end-to-end process review meetings (if not doing so already)

Finally, it's very important that the process leadership teams don't try to manage their process(es) in a vacuum! Process owners and members of their process leadership teams should be conducting regular meetings with their counterparts who have accountability for other end-to-end core processes within the organization to ensure alignment across all of the organization's value streams.

Approaches to Managing an End-to-End Project Portfolio

One of the key benefits of taking an integrated cross-functional approach to business process excellence is that it enables organizations to create an end-to-end process perspective of transformation and improvement opportunities, prioritize them appropriately, and determine which is the most appropriate methodology (such as Lean, Six Sigma, Kaizen) to realize benefits. This enables organizations to focus their transformation and improvement efforts on those projects that will generate the largest possible benefits for customers and shareholders. It can also provide process improvement-based developmental opportunities that are fulfilling and motivating for employees.

Without this perspective, organizations often find that their different improvement teams, however well intentioned, will not be sufficiently well aligned and coordinated to tackle the critical end-to-end process issues that truly create (or lose) value for customers and shareholders, and consequently their improvement efforts will be suboptimized.

Organizations that are able to view all of their proposed, active, and completed projects with an end-to-end core process mindset as a basis for taking a process-focused project portfolio perspective will have a key advantage over others.

There are various ways in which process owners and process leadership teams can review the *project portfolio* as part of their regular *process reviews*. We are going to focus on four key approaches that can be used. In doing so, we will outline how organizations can understand their end-to-end process project portfolio by:

- Process and subprocess
- Ease of implementation and value creation
- Execution timeline

The Process-Subprocess Perspective

A simple approach that enables an organization to understand the areas of its process on which it's focusing its improvement efforts involves the subprocesses. The organization uses the *process architecture* to map all projects against the subprocesses of the respective core end-to-end process—in the example in Figure 11.2, a generic customer acquisition process.

This "mapping" approach enables the organization to ask three very important questions:

1. *"Are we focusing our improvement efforts on those areas of the process where the data are telling us we have problems?"* For example, why do we have so many projects focusing on the "Signing New Customers" subprocess when our data are telling us that customers

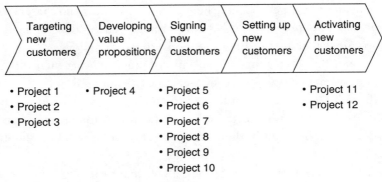

Figure 11.2 Projects mapped to subprocess

are experiencing major issues with the "Setting Up New Customers" subprocess? We don't have a single project focusing on this subprocess.

2. *"Are there any linkages or overlaps between projects that we need to be aware of?"* For example, we may find that the scope of Project 4 overlaps with the way in which Project 6 is currently scoped.

3. *"Do we have the capacity to successfully execute these projects in these subprocesses?"* For example, do we really have sufficient resources and change capabilities to simultaneously and successfully execute six projects in the "Signing New Customers" subprocess?

This perspective generally creates a very useful picture to spark discussion at the process review meetings and raise further questions about the organization's project portfolio. In fact, one organization has actually incorporated this model into its process redesign project for its monthly financial close process. It integrated design for Six Sigma (DFSS) techniques with its IT development plan to establish an overall picture of process changes throughout its organization.

The Ease-of-Implementation and Value-Creation Perspective

This approach involves creating a simple matrix[3] that can be used to plot the projects across the two key dimensions of ease of implementation and value creation (see Figure 11.3). Other dimensions that are often used with this method are risk and return, value and complexity, and scale and difficulty.

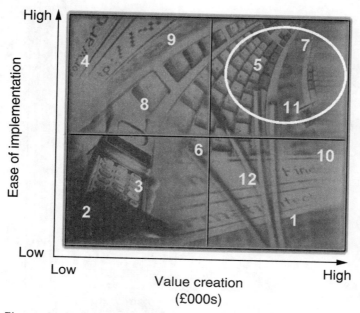

Figure 11.3 Implementation versus value matrix

This perspective can provide a valuable snapshot of an organization's project portfolio and is a good mechanism for effectively prioritizing project opportunities. As with the other portfolio review methods, this approach can also generate a large number of questions and considerable discussion at the regular process review meetings.

The Execution-Timeline Perspective

This approach is essentially a picture of the timeline for the proposed project sequencing—ideally framed within a multiyear plan (often called a *multigeneration plan*) that shows the planned journey toward the process POA (see Figure 11.4). As with the earlier tools, this provides yet another snapshot of the project portfolio that will undoubtedly generate further questions and discussion.

The approaches that we've shown in this section are particularly useful in helping organizations prioritize projects within their project portfolio. If you recall, the approach that Lloyds TSB took to its POTs (Process Owner Teams) was that they constantly *prioritize, prioritize, prioritize!* (step 7).

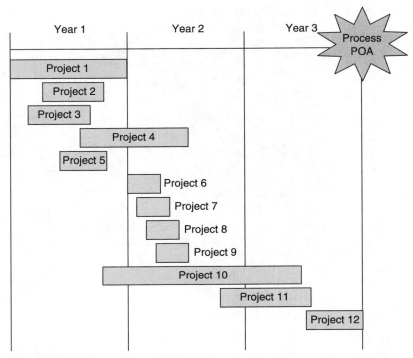

Figure 11.4 Execution timeline

If the last few pages have been a bit too theoretical for you, perhaps we could share a real-life example from one financial services organization that appears to have established an excellent approach to identifying and selecting the most important projects to work.

Citibank's approach[4] to selecting projects involves prioritizing problems based upon the volume of errors and complaints reported and the severity of the impact on the customer. This enables Citibank to identify the most problematic processes with the highest impact on the customer. The bank also looks at the occurrence of errors and complaints within the context of the overall customer experience to identify any channel failures. From this analysis, it is able to scope potential transformation and improvement opportunities for prioritization.

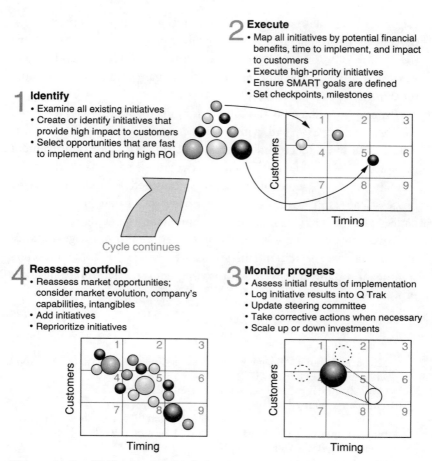

Figure 11.5   Citibank prioritization process

Citibank's prioritization process is based upon a nine-cell grid in which potential projects are plotted in terms of estimated project timing and customer impact (see Figure 11.5). The economic importance of each project (based on a COPQ[5] estimate of revenue increase or expense saved) is represented on the grid.

Closing Comments on Process Governance

The use of end-to-end process governance is an essential requirement of business process excellence and offers significant benefits to organizations that are able to establish the approach. Interestingly, only 36 percent of the financial services organizations that we surveyed view their various business improvement initiatives by core end-to-end processes today, with only half of these organizations also grouping their initiatives by subprocesses.

Process governance is the glue that binds together *process leadership* and *process knowledge*, and without which *process execution* is suboptimized. The most successful process transformation and improvement initiatives we have seen are those that relate directly to the business strategy with key stakeholders actively engaged as members of the process leadership team. Lloyds TSB has proved that process governance, while initially challenging to implement, can be done.

Given the current low levels of end-to-end process governance within financial services organizations, we believe this approach offers significant opportunities for improving and transforming business processes.

Notes

1. Michael Hammer, "Business Processes in Financial Services," Microsoft white paper (September 2003).
2. Critical-to-quality requirements (CTQs) in Six Sigma.
3. The matrix referred to is often known as a *filtering matrix*.
4. Alexis Goncalves, Director–Global Quality Intelligence, "Amplifying VOC through Innovation," Citigroup Global Consumer Bank, Six Sigma for Financial Services Conference, New York (July 27–28, 2004).
5. COPQ stands for cost of poor quality.

CHAPTER

Achieving Transformation and Improvement

There's too much waste in banking.
Getting rid of it takes tenacity, not brilliance.[1]

Carl E. Reichardt
Chairman, Wells Fargo & Co.

T HIS ENTIRE book is about achieving business process transformation and improvement, so you might think it rather odd that we have a chapter with this title. However, in this chapter, we plan to focus specifically on the key methods and tools that can be used to achieve *process transformation and improvement* at a project level. In doing so, we'll describe how some leading financial services organizations have used these approaches to systematically transform and improve their business processes.

Having utilized techniques such as the Citibank example in the previous chapter, organizations now need to execute their selected projects in the best possible way to deliver benefits to their customers and shareholders. Over 90 percent of the financial services organizations that we surveyed indicated that they have a Six Sigma program, and half of these organizations advised us that they have embedded Lean into their Six Sigma program.

With so many different methods, tools, and techniques available, it's often difficult to know which approach is best to use for which situation.

As one survey respondent wrote in *Quality Digest*'s 2004 annual survey of Six Sigma companies:

> *Six Sigma shouldn't be the only methodology; Six Sigma should be used when statistical tools are really necessary. Too often I see projects that could be resolved through a one-week kaizen event, but they're struggling to make a Six Sigma project out of it.*

In response to this challenge, some financial services organizations recognize and utilize a variety of different execution methods, tools, and techniques on a situational basis to maximize the impact of their transformation and improvement efforts (see Box 12.1). Up front project-specific information and extensive project experience are the keys

Box 12.1

Business Objective	Recommended Approach	Generally Accepted Method
"We need to establish some customer and process metrics for our core processes."	Six Sigma Process Management	DMAIC (Define, Measure, Analyze, Improve, Control)
"We need to fix this defect, but we don't understand the root causes."	Six Sigma Improve	DMAIC (Define, Measure, Analyze, Improve, Control)
"We need to completely reengineer this process."	Six Sigma Redesign	DMADV (Define, Measure, Analyze, Design, Verify)
"We need to develop a new product, service and/or operational capability."	Six Sigma Design	DMADV (Define, Measure, Analyze, Design, Verify)
"We need to speed up this process."	Lean	No standard industry construct exists.
"We need to fix this problem quickly. We've got the data telling us the root causes."	Kaizen or Workout	No standard industry construct exists.

Note: Six Sigma Design is also known as DFSS, Design for Six Sigma.

to enable organizations to select the most appropriate methodology for each specific opportunity within their portfolio.

In fact, some organizations are starting to use a mini preliminary Define, Measure, and Analyze phase as part of their preliminary project scoping work. The information acquired during this preliminary work is more comprehensive than typically is the case at this point in a Six Sigma project. With this understanding, project leaders are able to better understand each project's defining characteristics as a basis for selecting the most appropriate execution method.

"All Projects Are Equal...

...But some are more equal than others...." The various projects that organizations will initially identify through the business process excellence approaches we've described so far will not be equal in terms of their *scope, urgency, complexity,* and the *skills and knowledge* required to successfully execute them.

Figure 12.1 illustrates one approach that can be used by organizations to determine the most appropriate execution method, based on the scope, urgency, complexity, and knowledge characteristics of each project within their portfolio, in a more detailed way than described earlier. We recommend that each organization adopt a portfolio approach that utilizes the language of its own culture for successfully prioritizing improvement opportunities. As with the project portfolio perspectives discussed in the previous chapter, this approach enables process leadership teams to push their thinking and challenge their organization to have the best portfolio of projects. For example, if eight of the twelve projects are major Six Sigma design projects, how likely is it that the organization will have the required resources and capacity to simultaneously and successfully execute these projects? Probably very low!

Without doubt, the best project portfolios are those that are carefully balanced—containing different types of projects to mitigate any adverse risk.

As organizations mature in their use of these methods, they discover the types of projects that move swiftly and those that require more support; having a balance of these various project profiles can help organizations to deliver results continually and communicate success. Another

Portfolio of project ideas							

1. Scope							
a. The project's objective is to develop and implement a new product/service or capability	Yes	No	No	No	No	No	No
b. The project will address multiple issues*	Yes	Yes	No, single issue	No, single issue	No, single issue	No, single issue	No, single issue
c. The focus of the project is waste reduction and inventory improvement	No	Unlikely	No	No	Yes	Possibly	Possibly
d. The project focus is an EAM Level 1 or 2 process	Yes	Yes	No	No	No	No	No
e. The project is within the organizational span of control of the executive sponsor	No	No	Probably	Probably	Probably	Definitely	Definitely
2. Urgency							
a. The project must be completed within...	12–24 months	12 months	3–6 months	3–4 months	3–6 months	90–120 days	5 days
3. Complexity							
a. The project requires the involvement of numerous organizational functions	Yes	Yes	Probably	Probably	Probably	Unlikely	Possibly
b. The project is within a single geographic location	Unlikely	Unlikely	Probably	Probably	Probably	Yes	Yes
4. Knowledge							
a. The required data are readily available today	No	No	No	No	Probably	Probably	Yes
b. The root cause(s) is/are...	N/A	Unknown	Unknown	Unknown	Unknown	Highly suspected	Highly suspected
c. Statistical tools are required to determine the root cause(s)	N/A	Most likely	Yes	No	No	No	No
Recommended methodology for project execution	Six Sigma Design	Six Sigma Redesign	DMAIC BB led	DMAIC GB led	Lean	Workout	Kaizen

Determinig characteristic(s)

Figure 12.1

©2004 Roland Cavanagh and Rowland Hayler

factor that organizations should consider is the maturity level of the resources in utilizing these tools. The newer an organization, the longer initial projects generally take. All organizations typically experience some form of churn in their project portfolio, projects that don't pan out for one reason or another and fall off of the priority list. We have observed that those organizations that have learned this attempt to keep a B list of potential opportunities in their hip pocket to move resources to. It's very rarely a good idea for any organization to *put all of its project eggs into one basket!*

Tools, Tools, Tools

Well over a hundred different Lean, Six Sigma, and business process management tools are available to business process excellence practitioners. As with methodologies, knowing which to use—and when, where, and how—is a critical factor for project success and is often learned through experience. Those individuals and organizations that fail to gain this skill and "get it wrong" are likely to fail to fully address the issues they're looking to resolve. In short, they will not fully realize the benefits they had planned for, and the project will take much longer than it really should. It's also highly demotivating for employees. So, all in all, this is a situation to be avoided!

As organizations expand their understanding and gain experience of the various business tools and techniques that are available to achieve business process excellence, many develop the analogy of a toolkit, from which they can select the most appropriate tool or technique based upon the type of problem, issue, or opportunity they're facing. Interestingly, our survey of financial services organizations indicated that only 60 percent of organizations require their business transformation initiatives to utilize specific methods, tools, and techniques.

We like the analogy of a toolkit and have developed a toolkit of the top 30 tools that we believe are specifically relevant and applicable to financial services organizations. We've organized our toolkit into three "*compartments*"—basic tools (Box 12.2), intermediate tools (Box 12.3), and advanced tools (Box 12.4).

Before we take a look at each of the tool compartments, there are three highly important points that we would like you to note:

1. The tools listed are *not* the only tools that can be used, and equally there's *no* requirement to use all of them—although our *basic* list of tools is exactly that, and so we would suggest there's value in using *all* these tools in *all* projects.
2. The emphasis in using these tools should always be on using the correct tool at the correct time—if the tool's not right for the job, don't use it. Would you try to hammer in a nail with a screwdriver?
3. The order in which the tools are listed in each compartment is not indicative of their importance, but it does indicate the sequencing of their use within the overall project life cycle.

Now let's turn our attention to Box 12. 2, which presents the top 10 basic tools and techniques for financial services.

The intermediate tools, shown in Box 12.3, can be used in addition to the basic tools, depending on the scope, scale, and complexity of situation.

**Box 12.2   Top 10 Basic Tools and Techniques
for Financial Services**

Tool Name	Tool Description	Example Application in Financial Services
1. Project Charter	A form of project agreement that includes critical information on the team, the nature of the problem, proposed milestones, and the impact the project will have	Written for a project aimed at reducing defect errors in new card activation rates. This project has an estimated COPQ of $575,000, impacts customer satisfaction surveys by an adjusted 1.5 basis points, and is currently at 1.9 sigma
2. Stakeholder Analysis	An analysis to identify key stakeholders for the project, determine their degree of support, and define appropriate actions to influence as appropriate	Identified key stakeholders involved in the end-to-end customer acquisition process
3. SIPOC Diagrams and Process Maps	A high-level view of a process that follows a specific structure of supplier-input-process-output-customer and a vehicle for documenting the steps in a process	Showed the flow from vendors to employees for computer purchasing and distribution
4. Measurement Plan/Operational Definitions	A plan or definitions used to document which data are being used, where the data come from, and how the data are gathered and calculated	Defined all points of data measurement in the merchant credit card terminal installation process

Tool Name	Tool Description	Example Application in Financial Services
5. Pareto Chart	A chart that ranks the problems or problem areas in order of relative importance, helping to identify the critical few	Determined the most significant accounting categories that drive aged accounts
6. Run Chart	Looks at the pattern of the data in time sequence to identify potential root causes due to some natural grouping	Analysis of call handling time over an extended period of time showed significant differences by workers on one shift versus another
7. Cause-and-Effect Diagram (Fishbone or Ishikawa Diagram)	A diagram that is useful in brainstorming and organizing potential root causes of a specific effect or failure	Used to verify that all areas of root causes were considered in a technology online banking help desk project
8. Decision Criteria Matrix	A matrix used for prioritizing potential solutions using predetermined criteria that are scored based on their positive and negative contributions	Evaluated alternative software solutions for self-servicing Web site updates
9. Pilot, Test, and Implementation Plan	A planning tool used to help pilot and test a proposed solution before implementation and to document how the implementation will proceed	Piloted and tested a new straight-through processing system for direct settlement

(*continued*)

Box 12.2   Top 10 Basic Tools and Techniques for Financial Services (*continued*)

Tool Name	Tool Description	Example Application in Financial Services
10. Control Plan, Visual Controls	A document or plan that outlines control activities that will take place to monitor that improvement is being sustained. Should include actions to be taken if an out-of-control event occurs; often combined with visual controls	Monitored process to ensure charge dispute case resolution cycle times operated within specifications; plan also included specific actions to be taken when case volume or cycle time exceeded upper specification limits

Note: Six Sigma Design is also known as DFSS, Design for Six Sigma.

Box 12.3   Top 10 Intermediate Tools and Techniques for Financial Services

Tool Name	Tool Description	Example Application in Financial Services
1. Quality Function Deployment (QFD)	A prioritization matrix that is frequently used to link process measures to the customers' expectations, ensuring you are measuring the right things; it is also commonly used to link projects to measures and expectations, ensuring a continuous change from the customer through to the process	a) Validated that the right measures for a new product introduction were identified to ensure that customers' expectations would be met b) Used by the financial planning function of a large institution to determine which process had the most impact on disatisfied internal customers

Tool Name	Tool Description	Example Application in Financial Services
2. Value Stream Maps	Another mapping variant that clearly depicts how value flows through a process to the customer and identifies the associated time for all the steps (both value-added and non–value-added) in a process	Identified non–value-added steps and excessive wait times in a home loan mortgage process
3. Bench-marking	A technique used to evaluate like processes or procedures for best and worst practices	Identified best-in-class performance for statement printing
4. Kano Analysis	A technique pioneered by Dr. Noriako Kano to better understand customer requirements and their valuation of product features or services provided	Customers were surveyed to identify the disatisfiers, satisfiers, and delighters of the features associated with a credit card rewards program
5. Measurement Systems Analysis (MSA)	A group of techniques, including gage repeatability and reproducibility, that evaluate the quality of the data before those data are used to improve the process	Evaluated the validity of data from an automated report on transaction counts to verify accuracy
6. Process Capability, Cp/Cpk	A statistical measure used to determine if a process is capable of meeting the customers' requirements	Determined whether an accounting process could meet out-of-balance limits set by the internal auditor

(continued)

**Box 12.3   Top 10 Intermediate Tools and Techniques
for Financial Services (*continued*)**

Tool Name	Tool Description	Example Application in Financial Services
7. Failure Modes and Effects Analysis (FMEA)	An analysis that identifies a specific root-cause failure, the mode of failure, the effect of that failure, and the risk associated with its severity, occurrence, and detectability	Listed root causes for card acceptance failures, their failure modes and the ability to detect their occurrence, the significance of their occurrence, and the severity of each of those failures
8. Hypothesis, Correlation, and Regression Testing	A method for statistically testing the significance of potential root causes to verify the impact and relationships between variables	Validated the significant few root causes of cycle-time delays in account application approvals
9. Pull System (Kanban)	A system of integrating workplace flow of product based on signals from the next customer in the process	Improved the assembly and flow of sales brochure material
10. Statistical Process Control Charts (SPCs)	A series of statistically based charts that allow you to determine when variation is due to normal random chance or special-causes variation	Used to monitor daily file transmission delays

In addition to the basic and intermediate tools we're proposing, we have identified, based on our experience, 10 advanced tools that can be used to optimize a process on a much more selective basis (see Box 12.4). We are sure there will be some animated discussion among the more experienced Lean and Six Sigma professionals as to why we have selected these specific tools. We welcome such a discussion since we believe there is an opportunity for the financial services industry to reach out and learn from the application of advanced tools in other organizations.

In fact, some of the more advanced operations research and industrial engineering tools have been successfully used within the financial services industry for many years (e.g., advanced market simulation techniques within the securities and investment banking environment). Simulation allows organizations to create a visual map of the steps in the process and associated specific probabilities with each discrete activity. For instance, a branch teller can process certain transactions at an average of 3 minutes per transaction with a standard deviation of 0.5 minute. Customers arrive at a rate of 1 every 2 minutes. Simulation tools can help predict the probability of a customer waiting and for how long. The results can provide an excellent understanding of how an organization's processes will operate. Simulation uses many of the same statistical basics that many call center scheduling packages utilize to predict staffing needs.

Within the retail and consumer financial services industry there is currently a limited use of these tools outside of call centers, and they offer a rich opportunity for further competitive advantage. The challenge with many of the advanced tools is that they cannot be simply picked up from reading a help manual. Instead, they often require years of experience to master.

Several excellent software packages are available as well. Unfortunately their cost is usually directly proportional to their functionality and complexity, typically making it prohibitive for Black Belts to simply pick up the tool and apply it.

One of the key differences we have seen between financial services (or services in general) and manufacturing organizations is the willingness of manufacturing to invest in human research capital to apply advanced tools; manufacturers tend to better understand the value that industrial engineers can provide, and they readily recruit such resources to optimize their processes.

Box 12.4   Top 10 Advanced Tools and Techniques for Financial Services

Tool Name	Tool Description	Example Application in Financial Services
1. Conjoint Analysis	Allows organizations to determine the relative importance a consumer places on different features by comparing subsets of possible combinations; it is based on the fact that relative values of attributes considered jointly can be better measured than individually[2]	Used by a marketing department to compare credit product features for relative value to the consumer by different groups of customers
2. Data Transformation	A set of techniques for transforming data into a continuous normal distribution for use in hypothesis testing and other advanced analytical techniques	Transformed data on retail bank branch customer traffic into normalized data for further analysis
3. Theory of Constraints	A methodology for identifying constraints in the process and optimizing the flow to minimize the impact of that flow	Reduced cycle time for providing mutual fund investment prospectuses for customers
4. Design of Experiments (DOE)	A wide-ranging group of experimental designs used to define and evaluate relationships between different factors at different levels	Defined the critical factors and predictive equation for inbound call sales volume
5. Reliability Analysis	A way of understanding the rate at which things fail over time and thus how reliable they will be in	Used to manage the repair and maintenance schedule for ATM failures

Tool Name	Tool Description	Example Application in Financial Services
	application, usually expressed in Mean Time Between Failure (MTBF) or Mean Time To Failure (MTTF)	
6. Linear Programming	A tool useful in defining optimal combinations of resources to minimize cost and maximize profit	Developed advanced models for quantitative hedge fund analysis
7. Simulation	A technique that evaluates a process's performance in a computer-animated environment based on estimated probabilities of a series of discrete events occurring	Used by financial planners to model consumption, income, spending, and savings patterns for a client to demonstrate the impacts of current investment strategies
8. Total Productive Maintenance (TPM)	A tool that ensures that every machine in a process is 100 percent available	Improved ATM uptime and availability for customers to generate additional revenue for shareholders
9. Cell Design	A method for organization in the workplace to support pull systems and minimize waste	Redesigned card embossing process
10. TRIZ—Theory of Inventive Problem Solving	An approach used to develop potential product or process solutions based on a series of tables of known solutions	Used by a a financial services firm as part of a design for Six Sigma initiative to reduce post–call-handling time

So how have financial services organizations applied these various methods, tools, and techniques to transform and improve their processes? While some of these financial services organizations were unwilling to identify themselves with the projects below, they did willingly discuss various applications of business process excellence in their organizations.

Six Sigma Enabled Merger by Bank of America

Bank of America

There's probably no greater transformation project a financial services organization can embark upon than to merge with another financial institution. The scale and complexity of the operational and cultural changes required are often overwhelming for many organizations.

In 2003, Bank of America had successfully been using Six Sigma for over three years and was fully engaged in its merger with Fleet-Boston Financial, which had also been using Six Sigma for about a year. To the senior leaders involved, it seemed only natural that Six Sigma methods, tools, and techniques could and should be used to facilitate the merger process between these two well-established financial services organizations.

The project team involved[3] utilized the Six Sigma DMAIC (Define, Measure, Analyze, Improve, Control) construct and a variety of tools to enable the merger process. Hoshin planning was used to establish customer, associate, and shareholder goals for the merger. Kano analysis was used to determine specific customer CTQs. Graphical data analysis and process mapping were used to compare and contrast the "old" company processes vis-a-vis the "new" company processes, supported by an FMEA (Failure Modes and Effects Analysis) to evaluate and mitigate against risks. QFD (Quality Function Deployment) was used to assess the impact of changes and to prioritize requirements. In summary, all merger-related projects utilized the DMAIC construct and formal Tollgate reviews were conducted at the end of each phase, just as they would be in any other Six Sigma project.

To our knowledge, this is one of the first applications of such an approach to the merger transition process. As previously noted, in Bank of America's 2004 Annual Report to Shareholders, Ken Lewis, CEO, commented:

> *The merger transition process itself has been, without qualification, the smoothest and fastest I have seen in my career. From the beginning, we planned and executed the transition and all associated projects with strict adherence to a disciplined Six Sigma approach, improving processes, driving down costs and enhancing quality and productivity along the way.*

There are many poorly informed critics of Six Sigma who believe it can be used only on small scale, narrowly defined projects. This project from Bank of America proves that the philosophy, methods, tools, and techniques of Six Sigma can be applied by highly experienced resources to really large-scale transformation initiatives.

Six Sigma Design Project at a Global Merchant Acquirer

The merchant-acquiring business of a global diversified financial services organization recognized the need to drive significant improvements in its process for "on-boarding" new merchants. Millions of dollars were being spent annually signing up new merchants to accept credit cards as payment for products and services. Once signed, a high proportion of these merchants either failed to activate the process or submitted very low volumes of transactions. The organization realized that not only was there an opportunity for cost savings in relation to the merchant-acquisition process, but there was also a tremendous potential for increasing the revenue from new merchants.

The global head of quality chose to use Design for Six Sigma because he wanted to increase the focus on voice of the customer (VOC) and because the existing process could be improved only incrementally. The members of the Six Sigma design project team focused on the VOC feedback and completed a customer segmentation analysis of the existing sales data to drive a deeper understanding of the factors differentiating activation rates between potential merchants.

The segmented data clearly highlighted the factors differentiating two groups of merchants that were then classified as *high potential* and *low potential*. VOC survey responses also indicated that a "one-size-fits-all" process for signings and activation was not well received and was not meeting the merchants' various needs. Data also showed that various different merchants had dissimilar needs in the areas of training, technology support, and reporting.

Based on these data, a pilot program was developed with a tailored welcome package and other communications to fit specific merchant profiles. This program included a special emphasis and follow-up on those "high potentials" that failed to activate. After seeing a positive response from merchants during the test, the solution set was fully deployed, with results of over $2.5 million in cost savings during year 1 and an improved activation rate resulting in incremental charge volume profits of over $5 million for the initial 18 months.

The Lean Service Machine at Jefferson Pilot Financial[4]

Jefferson Pilot Financial (JPF) was a full-service life insurance and annuities company based in Greensboro, North Carolina. It has since been acquired by Lincoln Financial Group in Philadelphia, Pennsylvania. With rising customer expectations, the company had a proliferation of new products with ever-increasing complexity. The organization conducted an in-depth analysis of operations in its new business unit and identified several improvement opportunities, such as reducing variation in the processing of new policy applications, reducing cycle time in approvals, reducing or eliminating rework, and reducing the differential in cost per application between the processing facilities.

JPF chose to use Lean because the processing of insurance applications involves a physical or tangible product similar to a manufacturing process. A team was formed with five internal employees and three external Lean production consultants.

The team focused on creating a *model work cell* to operate independently from production operations to allow managers to experiment with various process changes. Within the cell the team placed linked processes near one another, used standardized procedures, eliminated rework loops or loop backs, measured standard processing times required to meet demand, and changed the work allocation process to a next-available process. The team went further to segregate complex applications from less complex ones, creating two groups. Finally the team used visual management to display the hourly productivity rates. The initiative cut the average processing time in half, reduced labor costs by 26 percent, and improved the quality as measured by reissues.

Six Sigma Improvement Project at a European Bank

This particular project was conducted at a highly profitable regional European commercial and savings bank. The bank needed to improve operational efficiency and first-pass accuracy in processing low-value wire transfer transactions—an area that had seen substantial growth, with approximately half of the transactions being manual paper based. EU banking rules prevented any increase in the fee structure for processing these transactions.

On the surface the process appeared to be operating at a very high level of quality, at over 5 sigma, or approximately 230 defects per million opportunities. However, the process was not cost effective due to the numerous inspection and quality checks required to operate and maintain this level of quality.

The Black Belt analyzed the types of errors that were being caught by the inspection process and that were causing rework. Using the Pareto principle on the collected data, the Black Belt was able to determine that 80 percent of the errors were caused at the point of origin due to either a customer or branch defect. There was high staff turnover, low productivity, multiple input forms (including the one prescribed by the EU), and unclear instructions for customer use. Data for each of these root causes were gathered, tested, and verified. On the basis of this analysis, the improvement team identified five specific areas for improvement:

1. Create a single form with a simple check-box-style entry for the customers.
2. Change the teller support software.
3. Reorganize personnel to ensure that work assignments match training in a more logical manner.
4. Establish better process measures to ensure control and provide input to future improvement initiatives.
5. Develop an e-training program for branch tellers.

While the final-results data from the control phase are not yet available, the total benefits from the project are estimated to be in the region of $2.4 million in the first 18 months. On the introduction of the new software system, a further $3.6 million in savings will be realized. This accounts for only "hard" dollar benefits and does not include staff-turnover–related benefits or cost-avoidance benefits in respect to increased transaction volumes.

Six Sigma Improvement Project at Barclays Stockbrokers[5]

Barclays Stockbrokers is the United Kingdom's biggest execution-only retail stockbroker, with 20 percent market share and 75 percent online  business. The team began its Six Sigma improvement project by conducting an end-to-end process review to identify areas of opportunity. It uncovered the fact that only 73 percent of clients requesting cash withdrawals from a trading account were receiving a same-day payment. This had a significant impact on satisfaction.

The team performed a Pareto analysis of the reasons for customers failing to receive same day payments. The main root cause emerging from this analysis was the existence of a cash system end-of-day cutoff time at approximately 4 p.m.; if cash withdrawal requests were entered after this time, they would carry over to the next working day. This system-driven time constraint had cascaded through the different client contact and its cash processing teams, who each had its own slightly earlier cutoff time in order to meet the end-of-day system time. The net effect was that some cash withdrawal requests received from clients after a certain point in the trading day would not be actioned until the following working day.

The leadership recognized that substantial systems and operational challenges existed in implementing changes to the process. The team engaged many colleagues across the end-to-end process, from client contact, operations, and IT to brainstorm, select, and pilot solutions to address the main root causes. The main solutions deployed were:

- Move cash system end-of-day processing from 4 p.m. to 5 p.m.
- Move each department's cash withdrawal cutoff to later in day
- Move Cash Ops and IT support shift finish times to later in day

The result of this effort was 93 percent same-day cash withdrawals.

A Kaizen Event at Fidelity Investments

In a presentation by Fidelity Investments given as part of the team competition at the 2006 World Conference on Quality and Improvement, we find an excellent example of how to hold a productive Kaizen event. In addition to being the largest mutual fund company in the United States and the number-one provider of workplace retire-  ment savings plans, it has become an emerging leader in the Human Resources Services Outsourcing business. This specific project was intended to improve service to over 3 million employees and retirees calling to enroll in benefit and health-care plans. The objective of this project was to increase the number of "one and dones," customer requests that can be completed during the initial phone call.

One of the three critical root causes was the capability of the representative to handle the different transactions. To break through the barriers caused by the knowledge gap in the Call Center, the team held a day long Kaizen event with nationwide representation from various groups in the Phone Center, Training Department, and Issue Resolution Department. The Kaizen event was a huge success, taking eight hours to achieve a breakthrough solution with training beginning the very next day for over 800 Call Center employees. The results were a staggering $2.1 million in savings, a 52 percent reduction in work items, an 18 percent increase in satisfaction scores, and the elimination of the need for mandatory overtime in the most critical enrollment period.

What's in a Label?

As has already been described, many financial services organizations are increasingly recognizing the value of taking a *portfolio* approach to their business transformation and improvement opportunities that enables them to use a combination of methods, tools, and techniques to address their business process excellence needs. In fact—and this is an extremely important point to note—it's highly likely that business process excellence efforts at financial services organizations will require projects to be executed using a number of different improvement, design, and redesign approaches, such as Lean, Kaizen, Workout, and Six Sigma.

Although the overarching term we've chosen to use is *business process excellence*, it's important to remember that the intent of this approach is to enable organizations to:

- Shape a process vision and strategy
- Establish process ownership
- Develop process capabilities
- Create the process architecture
- Establish process measurement systems
- Embed process governance

All of this is a means to identify the most critical business improvement and transformation opportunities. Once identified, they will need to be executed using the most appropriate methods, tools, and techniques on a situational basis dependent on the scale, scope, and complexity of each opportunity to achieve the overarching business process excellence objective for all organizations: improved business results.

It's extremely unlikely that any one method, tool, or technique will offer the best approach in all cases. To suggest otherwise is a bit like a doctor prescribing antibiotics in the hope that they will treat every ailment!

This concept is certainly well understood at ICICI Bank, which has developed a holistic, integrated approach to achieving workplace transformation, utilizing different methods, tools, and techniques. Here in summary is its story.

ICICI Bank[6] is India's second largest bank, providing retail, corporate, and investment banking services as well as insurance products and asset management. Despite strong financial performance following the merger of the ICICI financial institution with the ICICI Bank (its commercial banking affiliate) in March 2002, a number of challenges and opportunities required attention:

- Profitable customers needed to be retained amid growing competition.

- Service failures needed to be addressed (e.g., lead times).
- Productivity improvements were required as business volumes increased.

In addition, processes were continuing to evolve in some businesses, and in general, the bank's processes could best be characterized as high volume, labor intensive, and poorly defined, with a high number of defects leading to significant downstream costs. At the time, various improvement methodologies were being used across the bank—ISO, Kaizen, Five S, CMM, and Six Sigma—in an uncoordinated way.

The bank's approach to address these challenges, and to leverage the power of the various improvement approaches currently used, was to integrate all existing quality initiatives, improvement strategies, and key performance measures in a deployment model that it created and called *Workplace Transformation*. Essentially, businesses can use any methodology to meet their specific business needs, but it should lead to continual improvement.

Today, the bank views Six Sigma as a data-driven methodology to address chronic issues challenging the organization—an initiative for achieving real financial results by implementing process improvements using a set of linked and sequenced tools—and an enabler in its journey toward achieving business excellence (its words, not ours!) The bank's goal is to become a world-class organization leveraging quality practices compatible to business needs. While Six Sigma is recognized as a powerful approach, it is not the only improvement strategy ICICI can afford to engage in.

Closing Comments on Process Transformation and Improvement

This chapter covered many of the nuts and bolts of what people normally associate with Six Sigma and Lean, such as the different methods,[7] tools, and techniques that, when correctly used, can deliver demonstrable benefits to financial services organizations.

Knowing which methods and tools to use—and when, where, and how—are critical factors for project success and are learned through experience. All too frequently, Black Belts and Green Belts are daunted by the statistics and quantitative tools they are introduced to during their training and apprenticeship. For the most part, these tools account for no more than 15 to 20 percent of the actual improvement or change project effort. The "soft" tools, such as stakeholder analysis, required to successfully drive change, are equally critical—some would argue, more so—for achieving business process excellence.

As we have previously stated, those individuals and organizations that fail to gain this skill and "get it wrong" are likely to fail to fully address the issues they're looking to resolve. In short, they will not entirely realize the benefits they had planned for, and the project will take much longer than it really should. Project-specific information and extensive project experience are the keys to enable organizations to select and execute the most appropriate methodology for each specific project within their portfolios.

At the end of each successfully executed project, a part of the process and the organizational culture is changed. Tailoring the business process excellence approach to the organization's culture is critical for success.

Notes

1. "Managing: Carl E. Reichardt, Chairman, Wells Fargo & Co.," *Fortune* (February 27, 1989).
2. http://www.quickmba.com/marketing/research/conjoint/
3. "Six Sigma Enabled Merger," presentation by Jim Buchanan, Bank of America Quality and Productivity Transition Executive at IQPC Six Sigma for Financial Services conference, July 28, 2004.
4. Cynthia Karen Swank, "The Lean Service Machine," *Harvard Business Review* (October 2003).
5. "Delivering a 'First Class, First Time' Client Experience," Andy Steele, Programme Leader, Barclays Stockbrokers, October 28, 2005.
6. "Six Sigma in a Universal Bank," presentation given at the IQPC Asia Six Sigma Summit, Singapore (May 2004, presenter unknown).
7. For a more detailed look at these methodologies, we refer you to the references section at the back of the book.

CHAPTER

Fostering Culture

I N   T H I S   C H A P T E R, we'll explain the importance of a *business process excellence culture* and describe how some leading financial services organizations are going about establishing a culture that enables their business process excellence efforts to flourish and succeed. Since culture can be a bit of a "fuzzy" subject, we should start with some definitions.

At an organizational level, culture can be defined in a number of ways:

- "Organizational culture is the specific collection of values and norms that are shared by people and groups in an organization and that control the way they interact with each other and with stakeholders outside the organization. Organizational values are beliefs and ideas about what kinds of goals members of an organization should pursue and ideas about the appropriate kinds or standards of behavior organizational members should use to achieve these goals. From organizational values develop organizational norms, guidelines or expectations that prescribe appropriate kinds of behavior by employees in particular situations and control the behavior of organizational members towards one another."[1]
- "A pattern of shared basic assumptions that the group learned as it solved its problems of external adaptation and internal integration, that has worked well enough to be considered valid and therefore, to

be taught to new members as the correct way to perceive, think, and feel in relation to those problems."[2]

- "An active living phenomenon through which people jointly create and re-create the worlds in which they live."[3]

So, what is a business process excellence culture? We defined a business process in the very first chapter. To refresh your memory, it is "end-to-end work that creates customer value." Let's also establish a working definition for culture. In the *Oxford English Dictionary*, culture is defined as:

A particular form or type of intellectual development. Also, the civilization, customs, artistic achievements, etc., of a people, esp. at a certain stage of its development or history.[4]

For the sake of simplicity, perhaps we could agree that for our purposes, a business process excellence culture can be defined as, "The artefacts, behaviors, and symbols that exist in an organization to continually foster customer-focused end-to-end process excellence."

It's important to focus on culture because organizations that are able to establish and foster a continuous improvement-based business process excellence culture can achieve tremendous results.

We believe that three main areas need to be addressed to build such a culture in support of an organization's business process excellence efforts. They are:

1. Setting a vision for the type of culture the organization seeks to create
2. Assessing the current culture
3. Changing the culture to meet the vision

We hope the following examples help you see how others are attempting to build a Business Process Excellence culture within their organizations.

Setting a Vision for the Organization's Culture

At U.S. Bancorp, the culture of the organization is engendered with a service quality mindset.[5] With over 2,400 branch banking offices

across 24 states in the United States, the bank has
over 10 million customers and $209 billion in
assets.

U.S. Bancorp's view is, "Our Brand Is Service,"
and the bank has established a set of service guarantees, "Five Star Service Guaranteed—other banks promise great service.... We guarantee
it." At a branch banking level, this means:

- U.S. Bancorp 24-hour bankers will be available 24 hours a day, 7 days a week.
- ATMs will be available 24 hours a day, 7 days a week.
- You will wait no longer than 5 minutes in any teller line.
- We will respond to all questions the same day, when asked before 3 p.m.
- Checking and savings statements will always be accurate.

To deliver on these guarantees consistently requires the entire
organization to be continually focused on these core deliverables.

When many people refer to Lean or Six Sigma, they use phrases
such as "changing the organization to one that is data driven," or they
explain that they want "everyone to use the methods and tools in the
way they do their daily job." These statements are in many ways a vision
for the organization's culture.

Formed in 1988, Ocwen Financial Corporation is a vertically integrated, multibillion dollar, publicly traded financial services holding company, engaged in a variety of
businesses related to mortgage servicing, real estate asset
management, asset recovery, and technology. Ocwen started

its Six Sigma journey in 2001, and in a relatively short space of time
made good progress. In its 2002 Annual Report, Ocwen described its
approach:

*Six Sigma is a client-focused, process-oriented analytical toolkit that
establishes a disciplined focus on quality and efficiency. All of our technology and globalization efforts are now structured using the principles of
this methodology.*

In addition to the substantial financial benefits the organization gained from its more efficient processes, achieved through the completion of projects by the 280 or so employees in the United States and India who had received formal Six Sigma training at that time, Ocwen commented on the benefits that customers were experiencing from completed Six Sigma projects—benefis such as:

- Prompt and complete responses to all inquiries
- Improved access for borrowers to information on their loans from monthly statements, Ocwen's interactive voice response system, and the Internet
- More complete and timely portfolio data for investor customers
- Streamlined process to facilitate vendor registration

Ocwen's 2002 Annual Report went on to say:

While the specific cost reductions and quality improvements resulting from the projects we have completed to date are very important, equally important is the enhanced effectiveness of our people. Six Sigma makes our people better thinkers and equips them with the tools to bring effective and long-lasting solutions to all the business issues they tackle. This integration of Six Sigma into daily decision making is the hallmark of a true "Six Sigma Company" and the ultimate goal of our Six Sigma program.

In our view, the most telling comments are those that describe the broader benefits that Six Sigma can achieve for organizations as the methods, tools, and techniques become interwoven into daily operations, thus creating a new culture.

Once an organization has a vision for its business process excellence culture, and simpler is often better, it needs to assess the existing culture and respond accordingly. Each organization has a slightly different culture, and quite often each department is different. The way in which an organization sets about implementing and sustaining initiatives such as Lean and Six Sigma generally offers a very good insight into an organization's culture. The following example provides some fascinating insights into how Six Sigma was adapted to address the specific needs of the organization's culture.

Assessing the Current Organizational Culture

In the first part of our book we shared success stories from a number of leading financial services organizations that are striving to achieve business process excellence. You might recall that one of the companies we introduced was Countrywide, whose Six Sigma–based program called *FASTER* is generating significant results for the company. We'd now like to describe this program in a bit more detail[6] because we believe a large part of the success Countrywide has realized from its effort is due to the way in which it has uniquely adapted Six Sigma approaches to suit its specific culture and environment.

First, why does Countrywide call its program *FASTER*? What's wrong with the name Lean, or Six Sigma, or Lean Six Sigma, or Six Sigma Lean? (See Figure 13.1.) Countrywide describes its own organizational culture in the following way:

- No engineers!
- Many CPAs; auditor mentality
- Aggressively decentralized
- No trust of graphs or charts—that's "hiding"
- If it's a "project," it's taking too long!
- Cost of failure is (perceived to be) very low
- Profound results focus
- "I hate standardization. Flexibility is the key to our success"

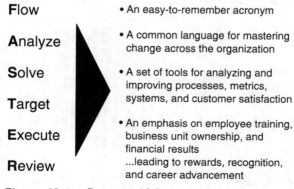

Figure 13.1   Countrywide's *FASTER* model

Consequently, to be successful, Countrywide's program had to focus on addressing these specific cultural characteristics.

How did Countrywide do it? First, it repackaged the Six Sigma methodology and put it in "CPA speak," and the company *didn't* mandate its use—that's because the organization has a history of crushing mandates. Instead, Countrywide earned the trust and respect of employees with a superior product that quickly demonstrated its power and value. Countrywide also created "pull" from senior leaders by surrounding them with their own people who were already highly enthusiastic about *FASTER*, the rationale being that as the program grows in complexity, the company can find the resources to absorb that complexity.

At the heart of Countrywide's success with *FASTER* is a solid understanding of the components that create and foster an organization's culture. Figure 13.2 depicts the importance of culture to the program.

The last point is critical. Incentives will be required in all cases to establish the new behaviors that a business process excellence journey requires. Establishing the appropriate rewards and recognition systems is a key enabler for embedding the new required behaviors (see Figure 13.3). Countrywide recognized how critical such programs can be for creating an environment of cultural change.

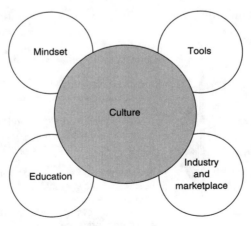

Figure 13.2
Organizational culture is at the heart of Countrywide's *FASTER* program

Rewards and Recognition

Platinum	Platinum medals are awarded to FASTER experts for projects that meet additional financial and analytical criteria and for mentoring other employees to gold
Gold	Gold medals are awarded for completing projects with audited financial results
Silver	3.5-day seminars engage employees in solving business problems in realtime
Bronze	Online training introduces all employees to basic FASTER concepts in 30 minutes

Awards are distributed by senior management at recognition banquets

Figure 13.3

Changing the Culture: "Buddy, Can You Spare Some Change?"

If, in it's simplest sense, business process excellence culture is thought of as "the way we do things around here," the examples from U.S. Bank, Countrywide, and Ocwen offer clear evidence that there are tangible, concrete actions that can be orchestrated to create the required culture. As Janet Young of Change Edge Consulting explains, enrolling people in the vision is the key to sustaining the momentum to ensure that business process excellence does in fact become the way an organization conducts its business. If organizations are serious about wanting to change the way things are done, new collective beliefs that in turn shape behaviors and actions are required. Having a concrete organizational change management process to deliver these changes is a nonnegotiable.

There are many models of organizational change management, and we certainly don't intend to get into each of those here. However, the theme that appears to unify these models is that "change is a process" that helps organizations move from defining where they are now *(current state)* to where they want to go *(desired future state)*, and it helps them shape the best way to get there *(transition)*. Thinking of change management as a process helps to outline the key steps needed to accelerate achievement of a desired culture:

First and foremost you must plan. Focus on a systems approach to your change effort—not just on what has to get done but how it has to get done and the context or environment in which you are operating.[7]

Adapting an Organizational Change Management approach is a structured methodology designed to increase the likelihood of success in managing the human variables associated with major change. Most models contain similar components for a successful approach including:

- Clearly articulated vision and point of arrival strategy for the business
- Committed leadership to translate the strategy into reality
- Assessment and alignment of organization systems to achieve business results
- Crafted communication strategy to build commitment

Organizational Change Management has targeted actions embedded in the project plan that help minimize the impact of the challenges that naturally occur in any transformation effort. Just as in the early phases of a Six Sigma project, one of the first stages in a change plan starts with a comprehensive data gathering effort on key organization systems and cultural elements, such as the readiness of the organization to commit to the transformational efforts, the level of resistance that might be present, the skill level of the employees to embark on this journey, the structure and business processes that may support or hinder the change process (e.g., reward and recognition process, decision-making processes, sponsorship, performance management process, etc).

It is a "pay me now or pay me later" situation, but you will pay—either through resistance and delays in the change effort or lack of active orchestration on the back end. Thoughtful planning on the front end, however, will mitigate the speed bumps that will slow down your change effort.[8]

The bottom line is, you can't "spare the change"; you have to "make the change" happen!

As an example of addressing change, we would like to revert to an example we introduced in Chapter 6—a process maturity model used by Roberto Saco, vice president, Strategic Planning, American Express. The following comments from Roberto on the pros and cons of implementing the PM³ model encapsulate many of the practical challenges of implementing end-to-end process-oriented changes in a historically functionally oriented organization.

Process teams and owners quickly understand the model and enjoy participating in the assessment exercise [Part of the PM³ program outlined by Roberto in Chapter 6]. Using color levels and a scoring board and toning down the technical jargon help to make the assessment a lively exercise. "Pinning the dot on the process" makes light of the affair, but the intensity and interest are evident throughout the day. Process owners like the combination of internal content knowledge and external facilitation, which balances differing perspectives and discourages gaming. So what's not to like?

Objections usually take one of the following five avenues:

- Subjectivity: *"But... it's all very subjective isn't it? After all, the scores are based on the opinion of the people who work on the process." The wisdom of crowds should not be underestimated. As long as there are representatives from various parts of the process and these people are knowledgeable (content experts), then there is enough intersubjective knowledge in the room to do the assessment.*
- Omniscience: *"You mean to tell me we need to go through this convoluted exercise only to 'discover' what I already know!" The counterargument is very direct: If you already know, then why haven't you done something about it? And if you already know, then why do you allow such a lousy process in this company? Of course, the fine art of diplomacy comes in handy when actually deploying these counterarguments.*
- Expertise: *"Given that the exercise requires knowledge of the assessment tool, doesn't that build dependence on a skilled and knowledgeable facilitator?" This is indeed a serious objection. One should not try this assessment at the office without due consideration to this objection. On the one hand, yes, any assessment tool requires a certain amount of expertise—in this case, my 15 years of assessing over 80 companies with similar instruments. On the other hand, our Master Black Belts took to the model and assessment exercise rather quickly—expertise can be built.*
- Results-only focus: *"If I have a comprehensive process scorecard in place, which tells me how my process is doing, why do I need an assessment model?" My counter here usually goes along these lines: Where is the relationship between means (capabilities) and ends (outcomes)? In other words, how did you obtain these process results, and how do you know that you can sustain them? Scorecards, even when well designed—quite a concession on my part!— are necessary but insufficient to attain process excellence. Periodically, a well-*

structured assessment allows process team members and owners to step back and look at a comprehensive picture of the end-to-end process in an exercise of recognition, discovery, and motivation.

- Length of time: *"You mean to tell me that we have to do this exercise in another year, and then maybe another year after that...this could take forever." This is the saddest objection, because it has no counterargument. It takes months, and often several years, of dedicated efforts to substantially improve the performance of processes (not to actually see improvements, of course). And, of course, existing processes have a history. Unless one is willing to make a sizable capital investment in totally new equipment or a brand-new facility, and pay additional moneys to have it installed in record time, that history will resist change. We don't like to hear this, but anyone who has had to clean up the aftermath of a quickly reengineered process will attest to it.*

Closing Comments on Culture

Our business process excellence model is simply about one thing—*achieving improved results* that benefit customers, shareholders, employees, and other key constituencies (see Figure 13.4). For financial services organizations to achieve improved results, it is critical that leaders understand how their organizational culture impacts, either

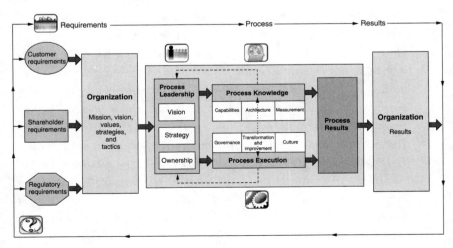

Figure 13.4

positively or negatively, the requirements of process leadership, process knowledge, and process execution.

Throughout the second half of our book we have focused on the key requirements for achieving business process excellence using the most powerful methods, tools, and techniques currently available. Each of those requirements if executed successfully will foster a customer-driven process mindset and organizational culture. This, in turn, contributes to a conducive environment in which organizations can continually achieve their business process excellence vision. This is a virtuous circle that many financial services organizations aspire to, but few, if any, have currently achieved.

Notes

1. Hill, Charles W. L., and Gareth R. Jones, *Strategic Management,* 5th ed. (Houghton Mifflin, MeansBusiness, Inc., 2001).
2. Schein, E. H., *Organizational Culture and Leadership,* (San Francisco, CA: Jossey-Bass, 2004).
3. Morgan, Gareth, *Images of Organization* (Thousand Oaks, CA: Sage Publications, 1997).
4. *Oxford English Dictionary,* 2nd ed., vol. IV (Oxford: Clarendon Press, 1989).
5. Richard K. Davis, president and chief operating officer, U.S. Bancorp, Smart-Tactics for Profitable Retail Delivery Conference, Las Vegas, NV (April 2003).
6. Jennifer Cohn, senior vice president–Performance Management Group, Countrywide Financial Corporation.
7. Janet M. Young, "Driving Performance Results at American Express," *Six Sigma Forum Magazine,* vol. 1, no. 1 (November 2001).
8. Janet M. Young, p. 20.

The Future of
Business Process
Excellence in
Financial Services

Introduction

In the final part of our book, we'd like to explore the future of business process excellence within the financial services industry over the next five to ten years.

To do so, we will peer into our crystal ball in an attempt to answer three important questions:

1. What will the financial services landscape of the future look like?
2. What are the organizational and operational characteristics that financial services organizations will need to demonstrate in order to successfully compete and create sustainable value?
3. Where is business process excellence heading, and how will it enable financial services organizations to successfully compete in the future?

1. The Financial Services Landscape of the Future

In the first part of this book, we provided our insights on the key drivers and emerging trends within the financial services industry. These factors are the driving forces for change that create the operational challenges of today and the future. The smart organizations are those that recognize these trends, their impacts, and the opportunities they create. These are likely to be the "winning" organizations that will go from "good to great" or "great to greater." These organizations are using business process excellence methods such as Lean and Six Sigma to successfully compete today and position themselves well for the future.

If you recall, we organized our driving forces of change around six key areas, reflecting a financial services organization's need to:

1. Continually satisfy customers
2. Create sustainable shareholder value
3. Comply with regulatory requirements
4. Address scale and complexity
5. Operate across an extended enterprise
6. Leverage enabling and accelerating technology

We believe that these forces will continue to drive the need for business process excellence across the financial services industry. So, how can we characterize the financial services landscape of the future?

Continually Satisfy Customers

Customers will become ever more discerning, demanding, and value savvy.[1] They will expect increasingly compelling value product, service, and rewards propositions. They will require the ability to communicate through multiple channels of their choosing. They will expect a single, high-quality touch point for resolution of any service issues. They will be extremely intolerant of mistimed and poorly executed cross- and up-selling. They will become increasingly mobile—ready and able to switch relationships quickly and easily. In short, the marketplace war for customer loyalty will continue to intensify, and the casualty count will be high.

Create Sustainable Shareholder Value

Shareholders will become increasingly demanding. They will become less tolerant of poor performance, especially compliance failures that damage the organization's brand and carry increasingly heavy fines. They will become significantly more aware of the causes of lost value, especially relating to costs associated with operational defects and waste. They will expect organizations to continually improve their efficiency ratios, and they will be unforgiving of organizations that provide "nasty surprises."

Comply with Regulatory Requirements

Regulators will become more powerful and more demanding. Regulatory reporting requirements will increase. The regulatory and audit framework will adopt an increasingly process-focused orientation. Regulators will direct more attention to organizations' offshore and outsourced operations. Bigger penalties will be introduced for regulatory compliance failures. In particular, organizations will need to strengthen their processes to address customer confidentiality requirements and to protect their customers from significant increases in ID theft.

Address Scale and Complexity

There will be continuing consolidation and rationalization among financial services organizations at both a regional and a global level. The emerging dominant players will look to leverage their brand position and achieve further operating economies of scale. The number and complexity of product offerings will continue to increase. New, initially small-scale niche entrants will compete on price and service differentials unencumbered by legacy platforms. Financial services organizations will increasingly evaluate, acquire, and merge with others based on Lean and Six Sigma methods.

Operate across an Extended Enterprise

Organizations will continue to offshore and outsource selective operations to low factor-cost locations (with an increasing emphasis on Asian markets such as China and Vietnam). A significantly greater emphasis on quality, data protection, privacy, and employee development will be required of service providers. There will be a shift in emphasis— client-vendor relationships will mature from simply *providing* to *partnering* as the delivery of additional ongoing value becomes more important. There will continue to be a few high-profile offshoring and outsourcing reversals where sustainable value fails to be achieved.

Leverage Enabling and Accelerating Technology

IT capabilities—people, applications, and infrastructure—will continue to align more closely with the operational strategies of the business to deliver tangible value. Shifts in customers' channel preferences will continue to create significant technology investment requirements. Organizations will continue to integrate their application portfolios to reduce cost, manage risk, and present a unified face to customers. BPM concepts will be increasingly used to maximize technology service delivery across customer-defined end-to-end processes. Those organizations that can successfully link Six Sigma, Lean, and BPM methods with their organizations' systems development processes will generate optimum returns from their business process excellence efforts.

Out of Left Field

While we believe the framework we have used to be robust, we recognize that discontinuous change such as political regime shifts—and unthinkable events such as those of 9/11—can and do occur. In dynamic global financial markets, these changes can generate immediate and unprecedented impacts and trigger other events that impact financial services organizations in unforeseen ways. Who knows what might come out of left field over the next five years?

2. Required Organizational and Operational Characteristics

How does this view of the financial services landscape of the future—assuming it to be even partially correct—translate into operational characteristics that financial services organizations will need to exhibit in order to successfully compete and create sustainable value in the future? Specifically, what are the business process excellence characteristics that organizations will need to demonstrate—day in, day out—in such a future world?

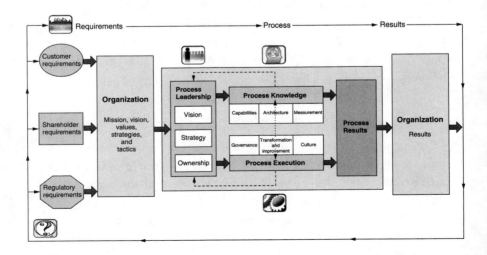

At the end of our first book, *What Is Six Sigma Process Management?*,[2] we sought to answer a similar question, and this is where our Business Process Excellence model began to take form. At that time we weren't thinking of the financial services industry specifically, but rather we were looking to identify general organizational and operational characteristics that would be required for any organization in any industry. As we researched this topic, we quickly learned that while many organizations are able to demonstrate a number of the characteristics we identified, such as Dell Computers with its world-class supply chain management and Toyota with its world-class production system, we were unable to find a single organization that could demonstrate many, let alone all, of the characteristics we identified—and no financial services organizations came anywhere close!

One could argue that we set the bar too high. Possibly, but we think not, especially based on the comments of one reviewer of our book, who wrote (and our sincerest apologies, in advance, for blowing our own trumpet here):

> *If I had to give a senior manager one chapter to read to see how to run an organization with a process improvement strategy, it is this chapter [Chapter 5]. I have seen organizations use only half of what the authors suggest and find extreme success in the marketplace. Just imagine what our economy would be like if most companies did most of what the authors suggest.*[3]

The point being that the model we proposed based on our research was being validated in the real world, and the financial services sector, by real business leaders.

Over the last year or so following the publication of our first book, we've further refined and developed both the business process excellence construct and the required organizational and operational characteristics we believe are required for organizations to compete successfully in the financial services environment of the future. As you review the characteristics we've identified, you might find it helpful to answer the following key questions:

1. Do I agree that this is a requirement for my organization to compete successfully in the future?

2. If so, is this organizational or operational attribute in place today? If not, what steps should we be taking to start getting this in place?

Process Leadership

❏ *Process vision. We have a vision for each end-to-end process, fully aligned with the business strategy.*
  - A customer- and key stakeholder-defined process point of arrival (POA) based on known process excellence and competitive benchmarking, fully aligned with the long-term strategic objectives of the company, has been developed for each end-to-end core process.

❏ *Process strategy. We have a structured plan to achieve our process vision.*
  - The core processes of the organization are highly valued and treasured as strategic assets.
  - Each process POA has been translated into meaningful, measurable, and aligned goals for each process participant (internal or external third party) engaged in the end-to-end process.
  - A multigenerational plan has been developed and is regularly updated to guide the organization's journey toward each of its process POAs.

❏ *Process ownership. We have a senior leader responsible for each end-to-end process.*
  - A senior leader has been appointed as the process owner for each of the company's core end-to-end processes. The leaders are equipped with the knowledge, skills, and resources to be highly successful in this role.
  - Each process owner leads a process leadership team consisting of leaders who represent each operational function, support function, and external third party involved in the end-to-end core process.

Process Knowledge

❏ *Process capabilities. We have the resources, skills, and capabilities to achieve our business process excellence objectives.*

- The process leadership team deploys resources within an end-to-end process context; e.g., Master Black Belts, Lean Masters, and Kaizen experts are dedicated to each core process.
- Human resource selection, development, and succession planning decisions are made within the context of the Business Process Excellence agenda.
- Career progression is dependent upon demonstrable (1) process improvement success using Lean Six Sigma techniques and (2) cross-functional leadership behaviors. A clearly defined career progression path exists within the end-to-end process—Green Belt to Black Belt to Master Black Belt to Lead Master Black Belt to deployment champion to process leader to process owner.
- All process participants have received relevant and applicable Business Process Excellence training for their role.
- Best practices are well documented and easily accessible to facilitate the transfer of best practices.
- Common process management and improvement vocabulary, methods, tools, and techniques are in place and appropriately used.
- There is a continual investment commitment (time and resources) to researching, identifying, and integrating leading-edge approaches to further expand business process excellence capabilities and maturity.

❏ ***Process architecture.*** *We understand our organization's end-to-end processes and how they fit together.*
- The relationships, linkages, and interdependencies between each end-to-end core process are fully understood.
- All end-to-end process documentation is held on a dynamic, easily accessible database with the appropriate change controls built in.

❏ ***Process measurement.*** *We have end-to-end customer-oriented process measurements.*
- A comprehensive, sophisticated, and diverse array of customer and process listening mechanisms is in place.
- A balanced scorecard is used for each core process to determine end-to-end process performance and progress in relation to the process POA.

- The balanced scorecard for each core process uses leading and lagging indicators that are empirically linked to the ultimate drivers of customer behavior for that process.
- The balanced scorecard for each core process breaks down into a hierarchy of measures that are seamlessly linked across and up and down the end-to-end process to facilitate performance management and problem solving.
- Operational definitions have been established and are commonly understood across the entire end-to-end process.
- All measurements are continually reviewed and assessed to ensure that the leading process indicators are correct.
- Measurements are continually refined and strengthened to ensure an up-to-date data-driven understanding of core process performance.
- All end-to-end process performance measurement is fully automated, with digitized real-time performance reporting available as required by each process participant.
- An executive information system is in place for the process owner and the process leadership team.

Process Execution

❑ **Process governance.** *We have end-to-end process governance and accountabilities.*

- The process leadership team (chaired by the process owner) meets monthly at a minimum to conduct a data-based review of end-to-end process performance, identify issues, review existing improvement projects, identify additional improvement priorities, and launch new projects.
- The process leadership team regularly meets with and listens to customers (existing, prospective, and lost); end-to-end process participants, especially frontline customer-facing employees; and third-party suppliers.
- Decisions are made using a consolidated end-to-end process portfolio approach to maximize value creation; investment trade-off decisions are made across the end-to-end process.
- All decisions are made using facts based on data.

❑ *Process transformation and improvement. We use leading methods, tools, and techniques to systematically transform and improve our end-to-end processes.*

- Project selection is made within the context of the end-to-end process, based upon what will have the greatest impact on ultimate value creation.
- A balanced set of KPIs is built in from the start of any new initiative.
- In-process feedback mechanisms alert process participants of any in-process defects prior to receipt by the customer.
- The visual display of process data facilitates the quick and easy identification of any out-of-control activities or performance.
- New products and services are brought to market with full knowledge of process capability and process performance measures.
- An automated change management process is in place to ensure that all process stakeholders review, challenge, and approve process changes before they're implemented.
- Process participants continually strive to make their process mistake-proof, making it impossible to do wrong.
- There is an extensive engagement of frontline and middle managers on project selection.
- Process participants are empowered to continually look for ways to improve the end-to-end process.
- Kaizen events are used to showcase and implement employee suggestions.
- Lean Six Sigma techniques are appropriately and continually employed to minimize in-process wastage, optimize inventory performance, and eliminate defects.

❑ *Process culture. We have an organizational culture that enables our business process excellence efforts to flourish and succeed.*

- The process leadership team continually fosters a key stakeholder-driven end-to-end business process excellence culture that transcends all functional boundaries.
- Cross-functional, end-to-end core process-oriented reward-and-recognition systems are in place. For example, process

participants are rewarded on end-to-end process performance; only a relatively small percentage of their compensation is driven by the performance of their own functional unit.

- The Health of the Process scorecard—focusing on end-to-end process performance—drives all reward-and-recognition mechanisms.
- Performance and results are communicated to the organization using the Health of the Process scorecard. A commonly held view exists at all levels of the process organization (end to end, top to bottom) about the process POA—how it's going to be achieved, where the organization is on the journey, and what the next set of immediate priorities are.
- All employees understand the process structure, the process leadership team roles, and their role in the process-oriented organization.
- Regular communication is provided by the process owner and process leadership team to process participants on progress toward the process POA—including performance results and successes, project updates, challenges, and opportunities.
- The end-to-end process environment is founded upon Lean Six Sigma principles, methods, tools, and techniques.
- Performance measurement, benchmarking, improvement, and management are the way of life.
- The end-to-end process environment is engendered with a continual quest for improvement at all levels of the organization.
- The leverage of solutions, knowledge, and best practices is encouraged, evident and rewarded.

In closing this topic, we fully acknowledge that the preceding list of "future-state" organizational and operational characteristics isn't complete. We're quite sure that others will identify additional future-state characteristics that we haven't yet thought of—and we're absolutely fine with that—we'd love to learn of your ideas. The point, however, is that, for many financial services organizations, achieving the degree of business process excellence just described will be a significant multi-year effort in and of itself.

3. Where Next?

So, where next? This is the question that many Lean, Six Sigma, and BPM consultants, practitioners, and commentators are frequently asked, and many are interested in finding an answer to.

While there are many perspectives, in truth nobody knows for sure what the future holds. However, there does appear to be an emerging consensus regarding the future direction of Six Sigma, Lean, and other approaches to business process transformation and improvement. Here's our take on it—in a nutshell:

- We expect to see a much stronger emphasis on the application of Lean– and Six Sigma–based mindsets and behaviors at leadership levels within financial services organizations. In the absence of such a much-needed development, organizations will continue to sub-optimize their deployment activities.
- We expect to see a continuing integration and blending of Six Sigma, Lean, and BPM methodologies with recognized and well-established assessment approaches (such as Baldrige and the EFQM models) to provide organizations with a highly robust pallet of business assessment, improvement, and transformation options.
- We believe that a much stronger focus on product and process innovation will emerge, as current techniques in general have yet to be fully integrated into a comprehensive approach to continuous systematic innovation.
- We expect the challenges and impact of globalization to continue, with the increasing adoption of Six Sigma and Lean methods across Europe and the tiger economies of India, China, and the Far East. We also expect to see the increasing application of Six Sigma and Lean in relatively *new industries* such as education, health care, and government.
- As the expansion we've described continues and the levels of application continue to grow, we expect to see further tools and techniques becoming aligned and incorporated into a coherent framework with existing Lean and Six Sigma constructs, such as DMAIC and DMADV.

In summary, we believe that business process excellence—an approach that links together the very best of business process management, Lean, Six Sigma, Kaizen, and other methods, tools, and techniques to achieve improved performance—is a fundamental requirement for the success of financial services organizations today, and increasingly in the future.

We very much hope that the ideas, stories, and suggestions contained within this book provide you with new perspectives on and insights into what business process excellence is and, more importantly, how it might be achieved within your organization.

We wish you every success on your continuing journey!

Notes

1. At the time of making final edits to our book, we were particularly struck by an article by Rupert Jones that appeared in the *Guardian* newspaper, London, on May 3, 2006, titled "Watchdog sees rising tide of dissatisfaction with banks," and felt that this article warranted inclusion.

   The article includes the following rather telling statements: "The Banking Code Standards Board [reported that it had] received 3,500 complaints and inquiries last year—providing fresh evidence of growing public anger and dissatisfaction. Between them, the big banks reported record profits of £33bn for last year, but they are facing a crackdown on charges and a growing outcry over the explosion in the number of cash machines charging fees for withdrawals."

   The article concludes, "Price comparison Web site moneysupermarket. com said the surge in complaints was "significant." "What is clear is that the banks need to be careful because customers are becoming more savvy in terms of shopping around."

2. Rowland Hayler and Michael D. Nichols, *What Is Six Sigma Process Management?* (McGraw-Hill, New York, 2005).

3. James Bossert, senior vice president, Bank of America, book review of *"What Is Six Sigma Process Management?" Six Sigma Forum Magazine* (August 2005).

EuroCountry Bank Six Sigma Case Study: Wire Transfer Process Improvement[1]

Gregory H. Watson
Managing Partner
Business Systems Solutions, Inc.

Introduction

EuroCountry Bank (ECB) is the nation's largest bank, based on deposits, and in 2005 it was identified through the media research as the most profitable business in the country. However, the bank did not want to sit on its laurels and realized that there were many externalities that were influencing its ability to maintain continuous, profitable growth and which were costing the bank too much in terms of operating costs. Faced with a pressing need to continue streamlining its operations and based on an assessment of its operational efficiencies, the bank decided to conduct a pilot Six Sigma project to demonstrate the ability of this new methodology to make improvements in the Treasury Department's Customer Operations Center.

Industry Background

Following the expansion of the European Union, a large number of workers from the new members have immigrated to reinforce the country's labor force. These workers have a strong tendency to send money home to support their families and have significantly increased the requirement of the bank to support "low-value" electronic fund transfers to these countries. In addition, the bank has acquired a large national bank in one of these larger nations and is positioning itself for future growth by specializing in the financial support of these emerging economies as a means to grow its financial services business.

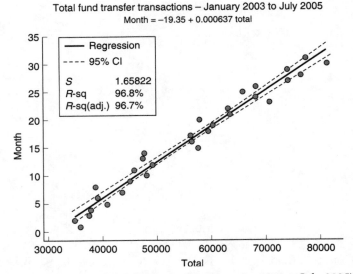

Figure AI.I. Total fund transfers (January 2003 to July 2005)

However, the low fees charged for these services (0.75 euro per transaction) do not allow recovery of processing costs (the initial request is completed on a paper form, and it is given to the teller) and certainly do not cover any costs of investigations or corrective actions required to assist in the transaction (often these forms are not even produced in English, and the funds transfer information may not be correct). Currently, the bank does not charge these customers a service fee for supporting failed transactions. To indicate the degree of significance of the problem, the base case for funds transfers was anchored at a period prior to an observed "runaway" growth in the number of these transactions, Figure A1.1 shows the volume of transactions up to the period of the Six Sigma project (from January 2003 to July 2005).[2] As observed in these data, the trend is strongly linear (note the 96.7 percent R^2 statistic), and the root cause of the problem has been traced directly to the number of immigrants who are transferring funds to their home countries.

Problem Definition

However, the problem is not in the growth of these transactions; it is in the cost to support the transactions due to the regulated fee structure as set by European Union banking rules. Since there is no opportunity to increase the fee for this service, the objective needs to be to ensure that the costs of the service do not exceed the fee. The problem as defined in the Six Sigma Black Belt project charter was:

- *Product or service.* Outward payments
- *Process.* Create, verify, and release payments
- *Baseline.* Current uncertainty on a daily basis as to likelihood of processing all paper applications for funds transfer at the desired standard of service
- *Desired status (describe project's target or goal).* Flawless execution of payment orders (100 percent) at desired customer service levels
- *Project objective.* To evaluate performance of the outward payment process and statistically characterize its operations to determine improvement opportunities
- *Projected business benefits (describe impact on customers or suppliers).* Increased productivity, lower unit costs, maintained customer service levels, and improved operational risk levels relative to the 2004 performance benchmarks

The cause of management's concern which initiated this project was based on the data, shown in Figure A1.1, that indicate that the total number of transactions (in the period of January 2003 to July 2005) was growing linearly. The Black Belt assigned to this project analyzed the forecast and recognized that continued growth in the observed trend (see Figure A1.2) was likely as the total number of immigrants continues to increase and the bank is still strengthening its own business position with these emerging EU countries. However, a business tension occurs in the outward payments processing center, where heroic efforts by the staff and a series of continuous improvement efforts have been barely able to keep up with the growth in payment throughput to date.

This problem is made worse by the fact that the growth in new transfers is split almost equally between paper transactions and electronic transactions (see Figure A1.3 for these data). The distinction between these two services is that while both are initiated by the customer, one is initiated in an electronic form and checked by computer software for quality control and managed through the transaction by computer processing (with manual checks for due diligence). The

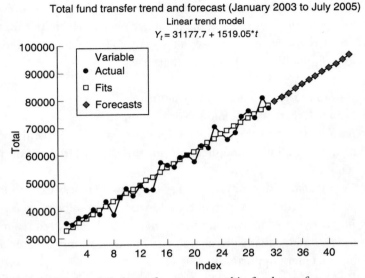

Total fund transfer trend and forecast (January 2003 to July 2005)
Linear trend model
$Y_t = 31177.7 + 1519.05*t$

Figure AI.2. Likely performance trend in fund transfers

other, the paper transaction, must be physically managed throughout the process, and it must be tracked throughout the system. Currently, the staff in the outward payments processing center are stretched to the limit of their productivity, and only an increase in staff size (and therefore the cost of this fixed-fee service) or a new technology that could streamline the operations (at an increase in capital costs for running the business) could help to relieve the problem.

The customer service center that the bank operates for processing payments includes two teams—one team dedicated to the processing of the transaction and a second team (which is more experienced and therefore more costly) focused on doing investigations for transactions that have failed to execute or have problems following release. Customer requirements for this work include the following considerations:

- External customer requires flawless execution of service request as defined by:

  - Right amount of funds
  - Taken from the right account (debit activity)
  - Transferred to the right bank

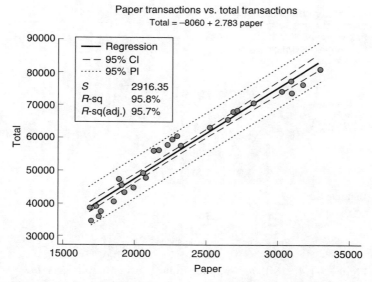

Figure A1.3. Relationship between the numbers of paper transactions and total transactions

- Deposited in the right account (credited to beneficiary)
- In the right currency
- Within the promised service-level agreement period

- Internal customer wants same flawless execution requirements, *plus*:

  - Meeting all regulatory and due diligence requirements
  - At the lowest total cost

- Measurable performance criteria:

  - Internal service target—process all payments same day of receipt
  - Service-level agreement—process all payments within 48 hours

To meet these requirements, the bank has set up the process depicted in Figure A1.4 (defined at a high level), with detailed performance definitions contained in supporting standard operating procedures (SOPs).

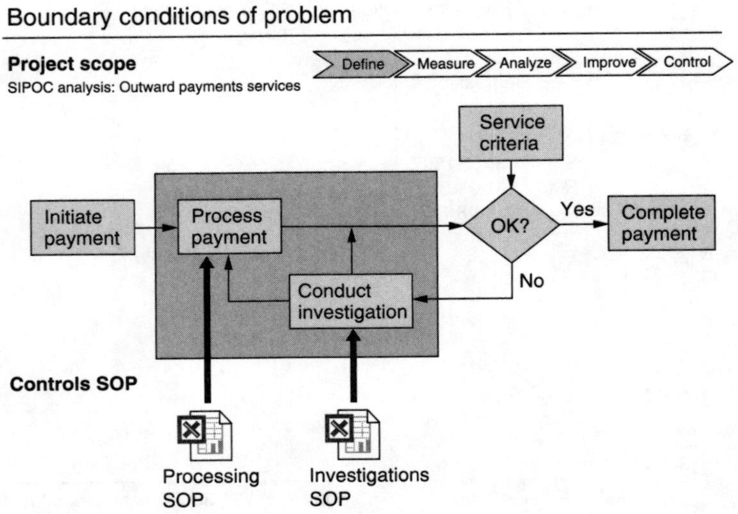

Boundary conditions of problem

Project scope

SIPOC analysis: Outward payments services

Define > Measure > Analyze > Improve > Control

Figure A1.4. SIPOC (supplier-input-process-output-customer) map of the process[3]

The management team decided to focus this Black Belt project in the following way:

- Limit the project scope to concentrate on payment processing improvements for paper transactions:

  - Note that there will be a secondary benefit accrued to investigations due to the influence of any improvements in processing which reduces its workload.

- Business measures (Y):

  - Productivity (paper transactions/employee/day)
  - Cycle time per transaction
  - Cost per transaction
  - Operational risk (write-offs)
  - Straight-through processing (STP)—those fund transfer transactions that require no human intervention throughout the entire process

- Desired state:

  - Service-level performance agreements optimized for delivery
  - Regulatory compliance fully met
  - Transaction volume increasing as cost per transaction decreases
  - Apply automation to minimize direct employee cost
  - Financial write-offs minimized (maintain or decrease 2004 levels)

Process Performance Analysis

As the Black Belt characterized the process using process mapping and measurement analysis of its performance, one key factor emerged (see Figure A1.5): The total number of electronic transfers at the branch level of bank operations has decreased by 56 percent when compared with the total number of transactions initiated over this period of time. Thus, while there are more transactions, the automated system is not being used to manage them! Thus, more of the burden of the new transactions is moving toward the paper-based transaction. This observation was further supported by information indicating that the majority of

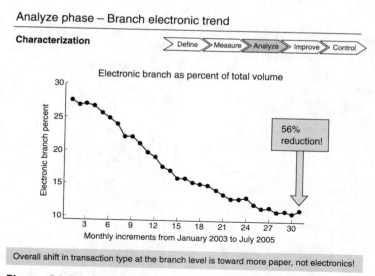

Figure A1.5. Trend relative decrease of electronic transfers as a percentage of total transfers

these new transactions were eurodollar transactions—the low-fee, EU-required transaction that burdens the system with processing activities which do not cover cost beyond the initial acceptance of the paperwork by the teller!

This analysis indicates that there is a basic need to work at the branch level to discover the reason for the shift away from electronic processing for the eurodollar product, as this product is one that should "require" electronic processing in order to control the cost of its support operations.

Consistency in Performance

The Black Belt also decided to baseline the process by calculating the sigma level of its performance. When analyzing the number of defects (investigations) in the total volume of transactions, it was discovered that the output of the current system is basically in a state of statistical control in a range between 5.0 and 5.2 sigma (roughly below 230 defects per million opportunities), with an average of 5.05 sigma (see Figure A1.6). However, the way in which this result is being achieved is not at all cost-effective, as the system-level quality is assured by multiple lev-

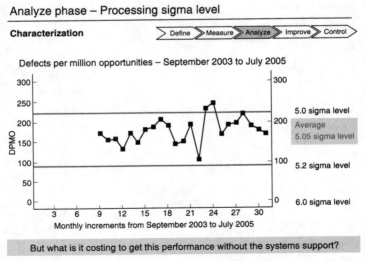

Figure Al.6. Sigma performance trend analysis for transaction processing quality

els of checking (inspection by in-process audits) in the process where both a second set of eyes and a third set of eyes—two more people checks—are used to ensure quality in outward processing. This greatly reduces the productivity of the outward payments team and increases its cost.

Risk Management

Risk is defined in this process as the cost of write-offs that the bank has to make in order to satisfy its service requirements. In order to understand what is happening in this area, the Black Belt analyzed the performance of the investigations team to discover what the reasons for failure were in the system. There were four major categories of failure that the Black Belt observed:

- *Customer.* Failures that occur in the transaction due to improper completion of the form, unclear handwriting, and incorrect or incomplete information
- *Branch.* Errors in processing the form that originate with the teller who initiates the transaction by not properly registering customer information
- *Processing.* Errors occurring in the outward payments process if people make mistakes in the transfer of the physical information into electronic form for submission through the SWIFT system for interbank transactions
- *Foreign.* Errors that occur once the SWIFT transaction has been completed by ECB

Figure A1.7 illustrates the results of the Black Belt's characterization analysis showing the breakdown using these four error categories.

The Black Belt noted that the Pareto principle holds true for this process, as about 80 percent of the errors observed were at the point of origin in the process and that they were due to either a customer defect or a branch-initiated defect. The Black Belt was able to trace most of these problems to a lack of compatibility between the data forms the tellers were using to enter the data and the software the tellers were using to record the transaction. There were four forms used, and the total number of fields on the eurodollar form was actually greater than

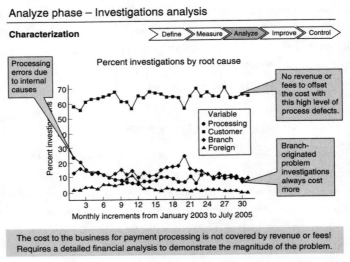

Figure A1.7. Analysis of defects by source of the problem

the number of fields on the forms that the bank tellers used for other types of fund transfers, so the tellers had a bias toward following the more simple procedure. In addition, the customer-originated errors were due largely to a poor quality of information about how the process actually works and the customer's own obligation to provide good-quality information about the transfer itself. These issues were identified as correctable through relatively simple software modifications that could be made to the bank's basic "money-moving" program that supports this process.

The amount of risk that the bank incurs was defined using two parameters:

- The number of credit debits to the total number of transactions
- The total cost of write-offs per million euros of funds transferred

The risk analysis of the bank's historical performance was analyzed as shown in Figure A1.8. While the bank was not satisfied with the current risk level, it was judged within a range that was acceptable for the service provided. Further, bank management noted that it had achieved a great decrease in risk at the beginning of this process observation period due to the introduction of ISO9000 quality controls and a basic

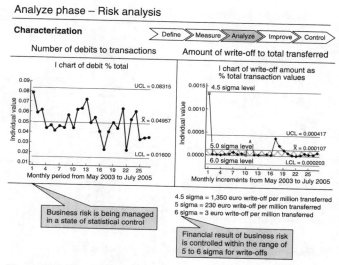

Figure A1.8. Risk analysis of the current process

process of continuous improvement. Indeed, the management decision to maintain the 2004 level of risk was based on those improvements previously made and the recognition that productivity was required to meet the bank's growth objectives through other services in order to gain an increased share of these emerging new EU financial markets. Additionally, any change in the process productivity would also simultaneously reduce the bank risk; thus the bank leaders agreed to focus on process productivity improvements.

Improvement Opportunities

In addition to the front-end improvements that could be made to this system due to either customer errors or branch bank–originated errors, there was also a category of processing errors that occurs within the outward payments team as well as issues about the level of payment processing productivity by the individual members of this team. One of the items that the Black Belt observed was that the turnover rate in this group (approximately 30 people) was such that the average tenure in the job was just under three years and that the more experienced people sought internal transfers to other parts of the bank that had less pressure and provided for more career mobility.

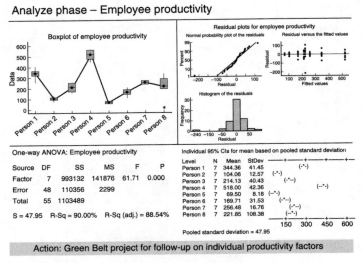

Figure A1.9. Employee productivity analysis

What is the impact of experience on the ability of the workers to process these transactions? To discover an answer to this inquiry, the Black Belt analyzed individual productivity. An example of the data is shown in Figure A1.9 for eight of the thirty employees. This analysis shows that one employee (identified as Person 4) had significantly more productivity (and when compared with error rates, Person 4 also had lower error rates), while two of the other individuals (Persons 2 and 5) had significantly less variation. The Black Belt noted that these were three of the most experienced operators. The low productivity and the tight variation of the two operators were due to the fact that they only handled "high-value" transfers (over 5 million euros), while the high productivity for the one operator indicated a specialty in a single type of transfer transaction. The remaining five employees in this illustration reflect the typical performance of this system.

Conclusions

What conclusions did the Black Belt draw from this study? There were five areas of improvement that were noted for implementation:

- Develop a single form for customer "money-mover" transactions that uses a check box to indicate the type of transaction, but solicit the same information for all of these transactions.
- Correct the teller-support software to make it easy to key in the critical information at the point of initiation in order to eliminate the cost associated with the subsequent paper transactions. Have the software provide error checking for the most common error types.
- Manage the personnel in the processing center in a way that optimizes training and the assignment of work in a more logical manner.
- Continue to collect process information and use these observations to help define the long-term software solution for both business-to-business and person-to-person fund transfers.
- Provide e-learning training for branch tellers to assist them in understanding the total implication of their work on the cost of bank operations and the need for "quality at the source" in order to help the bank continue its trend of profitable growth.

While the final cost savings of this project have not been accrued yet, it is clear that there is a tremendous impact in terms of cost avoidance. A reduction in errors for the eurodollar transactions results in more profit directly to the bank. And an increased level of productivity for the outward payments teams holds their head count stable and increases their productivity as the transaction volume increases, thereby avoiding future costs that would be required to support an increase in the number of operators. These savings are expected to achieve a significant and continuing benefit for ECB.

Notes

1. This case study is based on a large European national bank, which is indeed its nation's largest bank and also the country's most profitable business. For business reasons the bank's managers have asked that their name not be disclosed in this case study. While the name EuroCountry Bank is fictitious, the facts are all real.
2. This chart and all others used in this paper were produced using the Minitab 14.0 statistical software.
3. Figures A1.4 to A1.9 are from the Black Belt's final project report and have been edited to remove the bank's identity.

Financial Services Survey

Research Approach

Included within this book you will find the observations from our comprehensive survey on Process Management, conducted with 11 leading financial services organizations representing a mix of global and regional players offering a variety of financial products and services. The survey respondents were:

- American Express
- Bank of America
- Credit Suisse
- Dresdner Kleinwort Wasserstein
- First Data Resources
- JPMorgan Chase
- Lloyds TSB
- MBNA Consumer Finance
- Merrill Lynch
- Overseas Chinese Banking Corporation
- UBS

The purpose of the study, conducted at the end of 2005, was to:

- Determine the current state of process management maturity within the industry
- Identify specific challenges that organizations face in "Achieving World-Class Process Management"

- Identify examples of "world-class" process management
- Share specific, practical "best practices" that companies have followed.

The research effort used desk-based interviews, supplemented with face-to-face meetings or in-person phone interviews where appropriate. The research process the authors used is outlined as follows:

- Upon agreeing to participate, survey respondents worked individually to complete the survey contained within this document.
- A telephone or face-to-face interview was then conducted during which one of the authors would ask the respondents to communicate their response and clarify any questions and/or handle any required follow-ups.
- The authors then consolidated and tabulated all of the survey data.

The authors will not release any individual company data and have agreed to keep all responses confidential. The data have, and will, be used only for the purposes of this book.

Survey Structure

In addition to the normal demographic and company profile data one would expect to find in an industry-specific survey such as this, the authors created a series of questions based on the structure of the Business Process Excellence model used throughout the book.

In total, the survey consisted of 68 questions. What follows here is a sample of the questions used organized by key Business Process Excellence themes.

Process Leadership

1.3. Do you have process leadership teams (or equivalent) at your company?
   a. Yes.
   b. No

1.9. Has the process leadership team established customer-focused goals for the core end-to-end processes?
   a. Customer-focused goals are established for every core end-to-end process.
   b. Customer-focused goals are established for some core end-to-end processes.
   c. Customer-focused goals are being piloted or tested in some processes.
   d. No customer-focused goals are linked to the core end-to-end processes.

7.1. Is there a comprehensive strategy in place to develop, implement, and maintain core end-to-end process customer listening mechanisms?
   a. Yes
   b. No

Process Knowledge

1.1. Has your company defined its core end-to-end processes?
   a. At the enterprise level
   b. At the business-unit level
   c. Within significant business units only
   d. Sporadic or pilot use only
   e. No

3.2. Does your company use process-based scorecards to measure overall core end-to-end process performance?
   a. For all core end-to-end processes
   b. For some core end-to-end processes
   c. Not at all

5.1. Do your company's career progression requirements include the need for candidates to demonstrate successes in Six Sigma or Lean application?
   a. Always
   b. Varies by position
   c. Not at all

5.5. Is there a specific group with the responsibility for identifying new leading-edge business process improvement techniques?
   a. Yes
   b. No

Process Execution

8.8. Is a specific person, function, or organization tasked with the responsibility of driving continuous improvement in your core end-to-end process measurements?
   a. Yes
   b. No

9.2. Is there a requirement that all of your business transformation initiatives utilize specific methods, tools, and techniques?
   a. Yes
   b. No

9.8. Does your company have procedures in place to manage and communicate changes across your core end-to-end processes?
   a. Yes
   b. No

Please note that the numbering of the questions here is not sequential but represents the place of each question within the overall survey.

If you have further questions or need assistance in conducting a similar survey for your organization, please contact the authors at

info@sspm-ideas.com

Glossary of Terms

This glossary is not intended to be a comprehensive listing, but rather is intended to provide the reader with definitions for common terms that have not already been covered in the book.

Analyze

A phase in DMAIC and DMADV whereby process detail is scrutinized for improvement opportunities:

1. Data are investigated and verified in order to prove suspected root causes to substantiate the problem statement.
2. Process analysis includes reviewing process maps for value-added and non-value-added activities.

Assumption busting

A questioning process that helps identify, and eliminate, preconceptions that inhibit viable solutions.

Baseline measures

Data that signify the level of performance of a process as it is (or was) operating at the initiation of an improvement project (prior to solutions).

Brainstorming

A technique for collecting ideas from a variety of individuals in an open, free-flowing manner. Rules include:

No ideas are considered "dumb."

No judgments, discussions, or clarifications occur until all ideas are generated.

The wilder the better.

Business case

A broad statement of area of concern or opportunity that defines the impact or benefit of the potential improvement or the risk of not improving a process; links to business strategies, the customer, and company values; usually uses more global business language such as *customer satisfaction, market share, business profitability*, and *competitive edge*; not as specific as the problem statement.

Common causes

The influences on a process that are part of normal, everyday activity; common cause factors are usually harder to eliminate, as they require changes to the process. Problems arising from common causes can be referred to as "chronic pain."

Continuous improvement

Proactive efforts to increase quality, process performance, customer satisfaction, etc., through data-focused problem solving and process analysis as an ongoing activity.

Control

1. The final phase of DMAIC. After solutions have been implemented, *control* involves applying ongoing measures to track and verify the stability of the improvement and predictability of the process; often includes process management techniques, systems including process owners, cockpit charts, and/or process management charts, etc.

2. A statistical concept indicating that a process is operating within an expected range of variation and therefore is being influenced mainly by "common cause" factors. A process in such a state is said to be operating "in control."

Core end-to-end processes

High-level processes that are the primary drivers of value, satisfaction, and profit for an organization (e.g., customer acquisition, order to cash, purchase to pay).

Cost-benefit analysis

The identification of the costs associated with a solution and the estimated savings in order to determine the return on investment (ROI).

Cost of poor quality (COPQ)

Financial measures that depict the impact of problems (internal and external failures) in the process as it exists; includes costs for handoffs, rework, inspection, and other non-value-added activities.

Customer

Any person or organization that receives the output (product or service) of the process; can be internal to the organization or external.

Understanding the relationship between how the process impacts both internal and external customers is key to process management and improvement.

Customer requirements

Requirements that define the needs and expectations of the customer; translated into measurable terms that can be used in the process to ensure compliance with the customers' needs.

Cycle time

All time used in a process that includes actual work time and wait time.

Defect

Any instance or occurrence where the product or service fails to meet the customer requirements.

Defects per million opportunities (DPMO)

A calculation that indicates the amount of defects in a process per one million opportunities.

Define

The first phase in DMAIC and DMADV to define the problem, the process, the team, and the customer requirements.

Design

The fourth step in the DMADV process, when the project team creates the detailed level design and pilot test plan.

DMADV process

Six Sigma design action model: define-measure-analyze-design-verify.

DMAIC process

Six Sigma improvement action model: define-measure-analyze-improve-control.

Effectiveness

A measure related to how well the process output(s) meets the needs of the customer, e.g., on-time delivery, adherence to specifications, service experience, accuracy, value-added features, customer satisfaction level. Effectiveness measures tie primarily to customer satisfaction.

Efficiency

A measure related to the quantity of resources used in producing the output of a process—e.g., costs of the process, total cycle time, resources consumed, cost of defects, scrap, and waste. Efficiency measures tie primarily to company profitability.

Five "S"

> *Sort (seiri).* Identify unneeded items and move them to a tempo-rary holding area before deciding on criteria to retain or elimi-nate the items. Within a predetermined time, the items are disposed of, sold, moved, or given away.
>
> *Set in order (seiton).* Identify the best location for remaining items, relocate out-of-place items, set inventory limits, and install temporary location indicators.
>
> *Shine (seiso).* Clean everything, inside and out. Continue to inspect items by cleaning them, and clean them to prevent dirt, dust, and contamination from occurring.
>
> *Standardize (seiketsu).* Create the rules for maintaining and con-trolling the first three Ss and use visual controls.
>
> *Sustain (shitsuke).* Ensure adherence to the 5S standards through communication, training, and self-discipline.

Hand-off

Any time in a process where one person actually hands the item moving through the process to another person; potential opportu-nity to add defects, time, and cost to a process.

Improve

1. A phase in DMAIC whereby solutions and ideas are creatively generated and decided upon.
2. After a problem is fully identified, measured, and analyzed, potential solutions can be determined to solve the process prob-lem identified in the problem statement and to support the goal statement found in the team charter.

Input

Any product, service, or information that comes into the process from a supplier.

Kanban

An ordering information control "signal" that physically tracks the movement of parts and supplies and immediately informs the upstream process of downstream consumption; provides a signal for the upstream process to produce the product.

Lead time

Total work time + total wait time to produce a product.

Measure

1. The second phase in DMAIC and DMADV process whereby key measures are identified and data are collected and compiled.

2. A quantified evaluation of specific characteristics or level of performance based on observable data.

Moment of truth

Any event or point in a process when the external customer has an opportunity to form an opinion (positive, neutral, or negative) about the process or organization.

Multigenerational plan

A phased plan that shows the planned journey toward the process POA.

Non-value-adding activities (NVA)

The steps or tasks in a process that do not add value to the external customer and do not meet all three criteria for adding value; often include rework, hand-offs, inspection and control, wait and delays, etc.

Operational definition

A clear, precise description of the factor being measured or the term being used; used to ensure a clear understanding of terminology and the ability to operate a process or collect data consistently.

Output

Any product or service that comes out of, or is a result of, the activities within a process.

Pareto principle

The 80-20 rule, based on Vilfredo Pareto's research, which states that the vital few (20 percent) causes have a greater impact than the trivial many (80 percent) causes with a lesser impact.

Problem statement

A description of the symptoms, or the "pain," in the process. *Key factors:* usually written in noun-verb structure; does not suggest causes, solutions, or blame; usually included in a team charter and supported with numbers and more detail once data are obtained.

Process capability

The determination of whether or not a process, with normal variation, is capable of meeting customer requirements; a measure of the degree a process is or is not meeting customer requirements, compared with the distribution of the process.

Process leadership team

A team that consists of senior functional managers representing all internal company functions (and ideally external organizations) involved in the core end-to-end process.

Process management

The monitoring of defined and documented processes on an ongoing basis to ensure that measures are providing feedback on the flow and function of a process; key measures would include financial, process, people, and innovation.

Process owner

A senior leader who has ultimate accountability for the core end-to-end process. The process owner is generally a member of the organization's senior executive team.

Process point-of-arrival (POA) vision

A long-term, often aspirational, statement of how the core end-to-end process should perform; generally crafted as a set of five to seven key metrics or in some cases a few paragraphs.

Reengineering

The design or redesign of business; similar to process redesign, though in practice usually on a much larger scale or scope.

Rework loop

Any instance in a process where it is determined that the thing moving through the process has to be corrected by returning it to a previous step or person or organization in the process; adds time and costs and has the potential for creating confusion and more defects.

Rolled throughput

Sometimes referred to as *process yield*. The cumulative calculation of defects through multiple steps in a process. Total input units less the number of errors in the first process step = number of items "rolled through" that step. To get a percentage, take the number of items coming through the process correctly divided by the number of total units going into the process. Repeat this for each step of the process until you get an overall rolled throughput percentage.

Sigma

1. The standard deviation of a population.
2. The capability level of a process, measured as the number of standard deviations (sigmas) from the mean to the customer's specifications.

Special causes

Those instances or events that impact processes only under special circumstances—i.e., not part of the normal, daily operation of the process.

Standard deviation

A measure of the average distance that the values deviate from the mean, or the arithmetic average; calculated for continuous data only.

Supplier

Any person or organization that feeds inputs (products, services, or information) into the process; in a service organization, many times the customer is also the supplier.

Value-added (VA) activities

The steps or tasks in a process that meet all three criteria to define value as perceived by the external customer: (1) the customer cares, (2) the thing moving through the process changes, and (3) the step is done right the first time.

Value-enabling (VE) activities

The steps or tasks in a process that enable the work to move forward and add value to the customer but that do not meet all three of the value-added criteria; value-enabling steps should still be scrutinized for time and best practices—perhaps these steps could be done better.

Variation

The change or fluctuation of a specific characteristic in a process that determines how stable or predictable the process may be. Variation is affected by factors such as environment, people, machinery and equipment, methods and procedures, measurements, and materials. The object of any process improvement activities should be to reduce or eliminate variation.

Verify

The final phase in a DMADV; the final product design, production plan, and scorecard are delivered.

Vision

A statement of what an organization aspires to become and the groundbreaking things it would like to accomplish; should be realistic but focused beyond the "current reality."

Voice of the customer (VOC)

Data (complaints, surveys, comments, market research, etc.) that represent the views and needs of a company's customers. VOC data should be translated into measurable requirements for the process.

Wait time

The average time spent by the unit in queue, storage, in-basket, briefcase, file cabinet, computer disk, etc., when no work is being done on it.

Work time

The amount of time that work is actually being performed on the unit moving through the process (total of the work times for all steps in the whole work process).

Yield

The total number of units processed correctly through the process step(s).

Note: Thanks to Pivotal Resources for contributing much of this Glossary.

References

Here are additional contextual references that we have used in the development of our book, over and above those listed in the text itself.

Beecroft, G. Dennis, Grace L. Duffy, and John W. Moran, *The Executive Guide to Improvement and Change* (Milwaukee, WI: ASQ, 2003).

Breyfogle III, Forrest W., *Implementing Six Sigma,* 2nd ed. (New York: John Wiley & Sons, 2003).

Camp, Robert C., *Benchmarking* (Milwaukee, WI: ASQC Quality Press, 1989).

Cruickshank, Don, *Competition in UK Banking—A Report to the Chancellor of the Exchequer* (London, March 2000).

Frei, Frances X., and Patrick T. Harker, *Value Creation and Process Management: Evidence from Retail Banking,* research paper supported by the Wharton Financial Institutions Center.

Gale, Bradley T., *Managing Customer Value* (New York: Free Press, 1994).

George, Michael L., *Lean Six Sigma for Service* (New York: McGraw-Hill, 2003).

Harrington, H. James, *Business Process Improvement* (New York: McGraw-Hill, 1991).

Harry, Mikal, and Richard Schroeder, *Six Sigma* (New York: Doubleday, 2000).

Lawton, Robin L., *Creating a Customer-Centered Culture* (Milwaukee, WI: ASQ, 1993).

Levinson, Marc, *The Economist Guide to Financial Markets,* 3rd ed. (London: Profile Books, 2002).

Levinson, William A., and Raymond A. Rerick, *Lean Enterprise: A Synergistic Approach to Minimizing Waste* (Milwaukee, WI: ASQ, 2002).

Pande, Peter S., and Larry Holpp, *What Is Six Sigma?* (New York: McGraw-Hill, 2002).

Pande, Peter S., Robert P. Neuman, and Roland R. Cavanagh, *The Six Sigma Way* (New York: McGraw-Hill, 2000).

Pyzdek, Thomas, *The Six Sigma Handbook Revised and Expanded* (New York: McGraw-Hill, 2003).

Rantanen, Kalevi, and Ellen Domb, *Simplified Triz* (Boca Raton, FL: St. Lucie Press, 2002).

Soros, George, *Reforming Global Capitalism* (London: Little, Brown, 2000).

Watson, Gregory H., *Design for Six Sigma* (Goal QPC, 2005).

Watson, Gregory H., *Six Sigma for Business Leaders* (Goal QPC, 2004).

Womack, James P., and Daniel T. Jones, *Lean Thinking* (New York: Simon & Schuster, 1996).

Index

About the Authors

Rowland Hayler is a highly experienced business improvement consultant with extensive experience in successfully implementing change across a diverse range of financial services organizations.

His business improvement and global operations experience were gained throughout 15 years at American Express, during which time he served as the Chief Quality Officer for the international Merchant Services division.

Subsequently, as the Vice President of Six Sigma Application, Rowland led a team of Master Black Belts to expand the relevance, application, and results of Six Sigma across the American Express organization worldwide. During this time he led the in-house development of the company's Six Sigma Design methodology and curriculum, its Six Sigma Process Management approach, and codeveloped a set of Six Sigma Management Disciplines for everyday project use.

Since joining Pivotal Resources in early 2003 as head of international operations, Rowland has consulted on Six Sigma with many leading financial services organizations, including Bank Negara Indonesia, Halifax Bank of Scotland, Marks & Spencer Money, Marlborough Stirling, Overseas Chinese Banking Corporation, Swisscard, Dresdner Kleinwort Wasserstein, and UBS.

As a trained Master Black Belt, ISO9000 auditor, and Malcolm Baldrige Award internal company assessor, Rowland brings a valuable mix of practical business knowledge, strong leadership, and technical expertise in driving organizational change. He coauthored *What Is Six Sigma Process Management?* with Mike Nichols, published by McGraw-Hill in June 2005.

Rowland is a graduate of Goldsmiths College, University of London.

Mike Nichols is currently the principal consultant for Nichols Quality Associates, a consortium of Lean and Six Sigma Master Black Belts providing deployment consulting, training, and project coaching for business process improvement. Nichols's long-time interest in quality management has led him over the years to assume numerous leadership positions in the American Society for Quality, culminating in his service as president of the society for the 2007-2008 year.

Most recently he was the Director of Six Sigma Design and a certified Senior Master Black Belt for American Express, where he codeveloped the Six Sigma Design program (DFSS) and the Six Sigma Process Management (SSPM) curriculum. Additionally, he provided strategic deployment consultation to leadership, global training support, and managed a multimillion-dollar portfolio of Six Sigma projects.

Nichols was previously employed with Fed Ex, leading departments such as International Customer Service Engineering and Vehicle Reliability and Acquisition Planning. In addition to many other management, performance engineering, and analysis positions within Fed Ex, he was fortunate to be involved with many of their quality teams and programs, including their Quality Academy, Speakers Bureau, and the corporate ISO 9001 certification team. He was twice awarded the Chairman's 5-star award for performance.

Nichols is a Certified Quality Engineer, Certified Quality Manager, and Certified Quality Auditor by the American Society for Quality. On November 4, 2000, he was appointed as a Fellow of the Society in recognition of his contributions to quality. He has also served as a three-time examiner for the Tennessee Quality Award, and as an examiner and a two-time judge for the Greater Memphis Award for Quality. Currently he is serving on the Board of Judges for the North Carolina Award for Excellence.

Mike has both a Bachelors of Business degree in Finance and a Masters of Science in Industrial Systems Engineering from the University of Memphis. His teaching experience includes eight years as adjunct assistant professor at Embry-Riddle Aeronautical University–Memphis Center (teaching statistics, quantitative methods, and operations research), and as adjunct faculty at the University of Memphis, teaching production operations management. *(Go Tigers!)*